COLLECTION OF
G. SCHIRMER'S
OPERA LIBRETTOS

T0051174

MANON

Opera in Five Acts

Music by
Jules Massenet

Libretto by
HENRI MEILHAC and PHILIPPE GILLE

After the Novel by the Abbé Prévost

English Translation
by
GEORGE and PHYLLIS MEAD

Ed. 2540

G. SCHIRMER, *Inc.*

DISTRIBUTED BY
HAL•LEONARD®
CORPORATION
7777 W. BLUEMOUND RD. P.O. BOX 13819 MILWAUKEE, WI 53213

45550c

MANON

In the autumn of 1881, Jules Massenet (1842-1912) suggested to Henri Meilhac an opera based on the Abbé Prévost's novel *Manon Lescaut* (1731). The next day —according to Massenet's reminiscences—Meilhac surprised him with the libretto for the first two acts; and most of the ensuing year the two men, together with Philippe Gille, maintained a lively collaboration in the work on the opera. Massenet spent the latter part of 1882 at the Hague, in the very house where the Abbé Prévost had lived. Then, one evening in the spring of 1883, he and the librettists brought the completed score to the home of the director of the Opéra Comique, Léon Carvalho, where "between nine and midnight *Manon* was read" before the director and his wife, the former Mlle. Félix Miolan, distinguished lyric soprano.

When the Carvalhos had heard the score, they were delighted. Mme. Carvalho kept saying, "If I were only twenty years younger!" Massenet returned the compliment by dedicating the work to her.

By the time the opera was ready to be put in rehearsal, Massenet appeared with a copy of the vocal score already engraved and printed. "Well," said Carvalho, raising his eyebrows, "it is in bronze, then?" The more usual procedure would have been for Massenet to have waited until the opera had been revised in rehearsal. There was nothing for the director to do but play the opera as Massenet had had it engraved.

It was first performed at the Opéra Comique in Paris on January 19, 1884. Manon was played by Marie Heilbronn, the Chevalier Des Grieux by Talazac, Lescaut by Taskin, and the Count Des Grieux by Cobalet. The opera was well received and played for twenty-four engagements at the Opéra Comique, but the death of Mme. Heilbronn in 1885 and the burning of the opera house in 1887 prevented the work's being played in Paris for several years.

After the reopening of the Opéra Comique, *Manon* was revived in Paris with Miss Sanderson in the title rôle. She was still singing it there at its 200th performance. Its 500th performance on the stage of the Opéra Comique was sung with Marguerite Carré as Manon. Before Massenet's death in 1912, it had passed its 740th performance on that one stage.

Manon was first heard in New York (sung in Italian) at the Academy of Music on December 23, 1884. Eleven years later (on Jan. 16, 1895) New York heard it in French at the Metropolitan with Sybil Sanderson (an American singer, from Sacramento, California) as Manon and Jean de Reszke as Des Grieux.

THE STORY

ACT. I. In the courtyard of an inn at Amiens, in 1721, an elderly roué, Guillot, has ordered dinner with his friend Brétigny for three gay actresses, Poussette, Javotte and Rosette. While they dine, the swaggering officer Lescaut comes to wait for his young cousin, Manon, who is expected by the coach on her way to a convent. To the animated comment of village onlookers the travellers arrive, Manon among them. Greeted by her cousin, she describes the excitement of her journey. While Lescaut goes off to look after the luggage, Guillot makes advances toward the girl and offers his carriage, but is repulsed. Manon reflects wistfully on the gay life of his companions. By the time the handsome Chevalier des Grieux arrives, she is ready to yield to his rapturous love-making and go off with him in old Guillot's coach to Paris.

ACT II. Manon and Des Grieux are living happily in their Paris apartment, although the girl already conceals the fact that an unknown suitor is sending her flowers. Lescaut and Brétigny arrive, the former to demand that Des Grieux marry Manon, the latter to warn her that the young Chevalier is about to be kidnapped by his father and she had better turn instead to him. Manon lets Des Grieux go off to post a letter asking his father's permission to marry her. Sadly she bids farewell to the little table where they have so often dined. Des Grieux returns, dreaming of an idyllic life with his beloved. A knock disturbs the couple. Answering it, the Chevalier is seized by his father's emissaries and dragged away.

ACT III. The holiday crowd makes merry on the Cours la Reine, where the young actresses seek to evade their protector Guillot while Lescaut sentimentally addresses them. Preceded by a crowd of wealthy courtiers, Manon is ushered from her sedan chair by her new lover, Brétigny. Preening herself on her dazzling beauty and luxury, Manon sings a gay gavotte in praise of youth and pleasure. She is piqued by news which she overhears from a new arrival, the elderly Count des Grieux, that his son is about to enter holy orders. Learning that the Chevalier has grown cold to her charms, Manon pauses briefly to watch a divertissement arranged for her by Guillot; then she orders her cousin to direct her to St. Sulpice, where young Des Grieux is preaching.

In the dim sacristy of the ancient church, the faithful recount the eloquence of the new Abbé. Skeptical of his son's new virtue, the Count tries to persuade the young man to renounce his vocation and marry some suitable girl. Spurning his father's advice, Des Grieux falls on his knees to pray for strength to resist his memories of Manon, who arrives almost immediately. She is still too fascinating for him; again the lovers flee in each other's arms.

ACT IV. The Hôtel de Transylvanie, a famous gambling house of early 18th-century Paris, is crowded by pleasure seekers, among them Guillot and his three young companions. Manon and Des Grieux arrive, seeking to improve their fortunes. While the Chevalier settles down to a game with Guillot, Manon and the three girls celebrate their philosophy of living for the moment. Losing every hand, Guillot accuses Des Grieux of cheating and goes off to call the police. They arrive with the Count, arresting the young man and threatening his beautiful mistress with deportation.

ACT V. On the road to Le Havre, where Manon is to be deported to Louisiana, the Chevalier attempts with Lescaut's help to intercept the convoy of unfortunate women and rescue his beloved from exile. They succeed with a bribe, and Manon falls exhausted into Des Grieux' arms. She sinks to her knees and asks for pardon, murmuring that now she can die in piece. Her lover tries to rouse her, but, dreaming of their happiness, Manon expires.

Courtesy of Opera News

CAST OF CHARACTERS

THE CHEVALIER DES GRIEUX . . . . Tenor

THE COUNT DES GRIEUX, his father . . . . Bass

LESCAUT, Manon's cousin . . . . Baritone

GUILLOT MORFONTAINE, a nobleman . . . . Tenor

DE BRÉTIGNY, a tax-collector . . . . Baritone

INNKEEPER . . . . Baritone

TWO GUARDSMEN . . . . Tenor, Bass

PORTER OF THE SEMINARY

SERGEANT . . . . Tenor

MANON LESCAUT . . . . Soprano

POUSSETTE ⎫ . . . . Soprano

JAVOTTE ⎬ Actresses . . . . Mezzo-Soprano

ROSETTE ⎭ . . . . Mezzo-Soprano

MAID . . . . Mezzo-Soprano

Men and Women of Amiens; Travellers; Post-boys and Porters; Men and Women
of Paris; Gamblers; Guards.

SYNOPSIS OF SCENES

			Page
Act I	The courtyard of an inn at Amiens		1
Act II	The apartment of Des Grieux and Manon, in the Rue Vivienne, Paris		9
Act III	Scene 1	Cours la Reine, Paris	13
	Scene 2	The reception-room of the Seminary of St. Sulpice . . .	18
Act IV	The Hotel Transylvania, Paris		20
Act V	On the road to Le Havre		25

MANON

ACT ONE

The courtyard of an inn at Amiens. At the rear, a porte-cochère, opening on the street. Downstage right, a pavilion with balcony and steps. Downstage left, an arbor in front of which are a well and a stone bench. Beyond the arbor is the entrance to the inn.

(As the curtain rises, Brétigny is at the door of the pavilion. Guillot, napkin in hand, stands on the lowest step.)

GUILLOT *(calling)*
Hola! Hey! Innkeeper, come out!
How many times are we to shout
Before you condescend to serve us?

BRÉTIGNY
We want some wine!

GUILLOT
We want to dine!

BRÉTIGNY
Are you ignoring us on purpose?

BRÉTIGNY AND GUILLOT
See here! Will you never appear?

GUILLOT
For Guillot Morfontaine
To be treated with such scorn
Is too cruel to be borne!

BRÉTIGNY
He is dead, that is very clear!

GUILLOT
He is dead! He is dead!
POUSSETTE *(at the window, laughing)*
But getting angry will do no good!

GUILLOT
What shall we do, then?

BRÉTIGNY
What shall we do, then?

GUILLOT
He does not hear!

JAVOTTE, ROSETTE, POUSSETTE
The devil take him! We'll have to wake him!

POUSSETTE, JAVOTTE, ROSETTE, GUILLOT, BRÉTIGNY
Come on, Monsieur, there within!
Make us welcome at the inn!
Come and save us all from starving,
Or it's you we will be carving!

BRÉTIGNY *(listening)*
Well now, how now? He's still unheeding?

POUSSETTE, JAVOTTE, ROSETTE
He's still unheeding?

GUILLOT
He's still unheeding?

BRÉTIGNY
He is deaf to all our pleading!
POUSSETTE, JAVOTTE, ROSETTE
We'll try again!
GUILLOT
But don't forget,
All this will make us hungrier yet!
(The Innkeeper appears on the doorstep of the inn.)

BRÉTIGNY
Here he comes, after all!

GUILLOT *(in a ludicrous rage)*
Answer us when we call!

INNKEEPER
I to neglect a guest!
Your dinner's on the way
And all is of the best!
(A procession of servants carrying platters and dishes moves from the inn toward the pavilion with great solemnity.)

INNKEEPER *(importantly)*
A choice of hors-d'oeuvres . . .

ALL
Good!

INNKEEPER
Caviar canapé . . .
Poisson . . . poulet . . .

ALL
I say!

1

MANON

ACTE PREMIER

Le théâtre représente la cour d'une hôtellerie à Amiens.—Au fond, une grande porte-cochère ouvrant sur la rue.—A droite un pavillon auquel on monte par quelques marches.—A gauche, une tonnelle devant laquelle est un puits et un banc de pierre.—Derrière la tonnelle, l'entrée de l'hôtellerie.

(Au lever du rideau, Brétigny debout à la porte du pavillon, Guillot, sa serviette à la main, est au bas de la dernière marche.)

GUILLOT *(appelant)*
Holà! hé! Monsieur l'hôtelier!
Combien de temps faut-il crier
Avant que vous daigniez entendre?

BRÉTIGNY
Nous avons soif!

GUILLOT
Nous avons faim!

BRÉTIGNY
Vous moquez-vous de faire attendre?

BRÉTIGNY, GUILLOT
Morbleu! Viendrez-vous à la fin?

GUILLOT
Foi de Guillot Morfontaine!
C'est par trop de cruauté
Pour des gens de qualité!

BRÉTIGNY
Il est mort, la chose est certaine!

GUILLOT
Il est mort! Il est mort!

POUSSETTE *(à la fenêtre)*
Allons, messieurs, point de courroux!

GUILLOT
Que faut-il faire?

BRÉTIGNY
Que faut-il faire?

GUILLOT
Il n'entends pas!

JAVOTTE, POUSSETTE, ROSETTE
On le rappelle! on le harcelle!

JAVOTTE, POUSSETTE, ROSETTE, BRÉTIGNY, GUILLOT
Voyons, monsieur l'hôtelier,
Montrez-vous hospitalier!
Sauvez-nous de la famine,
Si non l'on vous extermine!

BRÉTIGNY *(écoutant)*
Eh bien! . . . Eh quoi! . . . pas de réponse?

POUSSETTE, JAVOTTE, ROSETTE
Pas de réponse?

GUILLOT
Pas de réponse?

BRÉTIGNY
Il est sourd à notre semonce!

POUSSETTE, JAVOTTE, ROSETTE
Recommençons!

GUILLOT
Pas trop de bruit!
Cela redouble l'appétit!
(L'Hôtelier sur le pas de sa porte)

BRÉTIGNY
Ah! Voilà le coupable!

GUILLOT
Réponds-nous, misérable!

L'HOTELIER
Moi! vous abandonner!
Je ne dirai qu'un mot: Qu'on serve le diner!

(A ce moment, des marmitons sortent de l'hôtellerie en portant des plats, ils se dirigent lentement et presque solennellement vers le pavillon.)

L'HOTELIER *(avec importance)*
Hors-d'oeuvres de choix . . .

TOUS
Bien!

L'HOTELIER
Et diverses épices . . .
Poisson, poulet . . .

TOUS
Parfait!

JAVOTTE

What a fish!

GUILLOT

What a dish!

BRÉTIGNY

Hurray!

POUSSETTE

Oh sweet and kindly fortune!

ALL

Dinner's on the way!

INNKEEPER (*persisting*)

There is beef, there is lobster . . . .

ALL

Look at the lobster!

INNKEEPER

All the proper wines
And all beyond compare!

GUILLOT

Handle them with care!

INNKEEPER

And the final touch to the banquet
Is a goose liver tart!

ALL

Liver tart!

INNKEEPER (*bridling*)

No, no, Messieurs! A work of art!

GUILLOT

Of course!

BRÉTIGNY

Of course!

ALL

Oh sweet and kindly fortune!
Dinner's on the way!
Now at last we're greeted
By the welcome call
Bidding one and all "Be seated!
Dinner's on the way!"
  Be seated!

INNKEEPER

Now that you are greeted
By the welcome call,
Hungry people all,
Won't you please be seated!
Dinner's on the way!
  Be seated!

(*The waiters and guests go into the pavilion. The Innkeeper remains in the courtyard.*)

INNKEEPER

It's all very well for them to order dinner, if they can pay for it. I'm going —but wait— The Chevalier Des Grieux! I promised to reserve him a seat in the first coach!

(*He sees the villagers about to crowd into the inn.*)

Here comes the usual crowd of my fellow-townsmen, hoping to get a look at some pretty girl, or to make fun of the travelers as they come and go.
The human race will always run to see a show.

(*He goes into the office. The inn clock strikes. The crowd drifts into the courtyard.*)

THE VILLAGERS

Now that the time is nearing
And the coach is appearing,
We must see all, see all!
See who will come, the men and ladies,
See who will go!
Ah, yes! This we must know!

(*Lescaut enters, followed by two guardsmen.*)

LESCAUT (*to the guardsmen*)

Is this the inn? Is this the station where the coach from Arras very soon will arrive?

GUARDSMEN

This is the place.

LESCAUT (*dismissing them*)

Goodbye.

GUARDSMEN

Surely you must be joking, Lescaut.
Are you leaving us now?

LESCAUT

No, no!
You two can go straight to the inn
Where the claret is old and fine.
I will wait here to meet my cousin
And then we'll have plenty of wine.

GUARDSMEN

Do not forget!

LESCAUT (*offended*)

Me, forget? That is an insult!

GUARDSMEN (*suppliantly*)

Lescaut!

JAVOTTE
Du poisson!

GUILLOT
Du poulet!

BRÉTIGNY
Parfait!

POUSSETTE
Ô douce providence!

TOUS
On vient nous servir!

L'HOTELIER
Un buisson d'écrevisses!

TOUS
Des écrevisses!

L'HOTELIER
Et pour arroser le repas,
De vieux vins!

GUILLOT
Ne les troublez pas!

L'HOTELIER
Et pour compléter les services,
Le pâté de canard!

TOUS
Un pâté!

L'HOTELIER (se rengorgeant)
Non pas, messieurs! Un objet d'art!

GUILLOT
Vraiment!

BRÉTIGNY
Parfait!

BRÉTIGNY, GUILLOT, LES FEMMES
Ô douce providence,
Voilà qu'en cadence,
On vient nous servir!
Ô sort délectable,
Lorsque l'on a faim,
De se mettre enfin,
A table!
A table!

L'HOTELIER
Voyez! On vient vous servir!
Il est préférable,
Et même très sain,
D'attendre la faim
Mettez vous à table!
A table!

(Ils rentrent dans le pavillon dont la
   fenêtre et la porte se referment.)

L'HOTELIER
C'est très bien de dîner! Il faut aussi
   payer! Et je vais . . . Mais au fait,
   pensons au Chevalier Des Grieux! Le
   temps passe, et j'ai promis de retenir
   sa place au premier coche.

(Les bourgeois commencent à envahir
   la scène.)

Et mais, voilà, déjà la ribambelle des
   bons bourgeois! Ils viennent regarder
   si l'on peut lorgner quelque belle, ou
   se moquer de quelque voyageur!
J'ai remarqué que l'homme est très
   observateur!

(Il entre dans le bureau.)

LE CHOEUR DES BOURGEOIS
(entrant au son d'une cloche)
Entendez-vous la cloche,
Voici l'heure du coche!
Il faut tout voir! tout voir!
Les voyageurs, les voyageuses,
Il faut tout voir!
Pour nous c'est un devoir!

LESCAUT (entrant avec deux gardes)
C'est bien ici l'hôtellerie
Où le coche d'Arras va tantôt s'ar-
   rêter?

LES GARDES
C'est bien ici!

LESCAUT (les congédiant)
Bonsoir!

LES GARDES
Quelle plaisanterie!
Lescaut, tu pourrais nous quitter!

LESCAUT
Jamais! Allez à l'auberge voisine;
On y vend un clairet joyeaux;
Je vais attendre ma cousine,
Et je vous rejoins tous les deux!

LES GARDES
Rappelle-toi!

LESCAUT
Vous m'insultez, c'est imprudent!

LES GARDES
Lescaut!

LESCAUT (*pleased and arrogant*)
All right! I'll forget what I've been
  thinking
When we get down to drinking.
You two go and drink while you wait,
Go on and drink!
(*The street fills with post-boys and
  porters carrying boxes and luggage,
  preceded by travellers of both sexes,
  who mill about in search of their
  possessions.*)

VILLAGERS (*happily*)
Here they are! Here they are! Here
  they are!
(*The coach is seen upstage. The last of
  the passengers get out.*)

AN OLD LADY (*tidying herself*)
My clothes are mussy! My hair-pins are
  falling!

CHORUS OF VILLAGERS (*laughing*)
The poor old thing is too appalling!

ANOTHER TRAVELLER
Boy, where's my bag?

A PORTER (*rudely*)
You'll have to wait!

CHORUS
Ah, there's a funny-looking creature!

A LADY TRAVELLER
Who has seen my birds and my bird-
  cage?

A MAN
Boy! Where's the boy?

A WOMAN
Where's the boy?

ANOTHER MAN
Hey! Where's the boy?

ANOTHER WOMAN
Where's the boy?

A MAN
My parcel!

A WOMAN
Where's my purse!

ALL THE MEN
Where's the boy?

ALL THE WOMEN
Where's the boy?

POST-BOYS AND PORTERS
(*sorting things out*)
You'll get your luggage,
Don't you worry.

ALL TOGETHER
We want our baggage in a hurry!

PORTERS
Don't try to rush us!

TRAVELLERS
Come on! Come on!

PORTERS
No, no, no, no!

TRAVELLERS
Ah! When you travel in a coach
  Or in a carriage or a cart,
Oh! Take my very good advice
  And make your will before you start!

PORTERS AND POST-BOYS
Ah! People riding in a coach
  Are in a temper from the start!
Oh! They are moaning when they meet
  you,
They are groaning when they part!

VILLAGERS
Ah! When they travel in the coach
  They moan and groan.
Oh! They are moaning when they meet
  And when they part!

TRAVELLERS
(*running after the Post-boys*)
I am the first!

POST-BOYS (*rudely*)
You'll be last!

VILLAGERS (*mimicking the Post-boys*)
You'll be last!

TRAVELLERS
I am first!

POST-BOYS AND VILLAGERS
No!
(*Manon has come out of the crowd
  and watches all the commotion with
  astonishment.*)

LESCAUT (*observing her*)
I should imagine that yonder lovely
  lass is my cousin Manon.
(*approaches her*)
I am Lescaut.

LESCAUT

C'est bon! Je perdrais la mémoire
Quand il s'agit de boire!
Allez! à l'auberge voisine,
On y vend un clairet joyeux!
Allez trinquer en m'attendant!

(*La rue se remplie de postillons et de porteurs chargés de malles, de cartons, de valises, et précédés d'une foule de voyageurs et de voyageuses qui tournent autour d'eux pour obtenir leurs bagages.*)

LES BOURGEOIS (*avec joie*)

Ah! les voilà! Les voilà!

UNE VIEILLE DAME (*se rajustant*)

Oh! ma coiffure! Oh! ma toilette!

LE CHOEUR (*riant*)

Voyez-vous pas cette coquette!

UN VOYAGEUR

Hé! le porteur!

LE PORTEUR

Dans un instant!

LE CHOEUR

Ah! le singulier personnage!

UNE VOYAGEUSE

Où sont mes oiseaux et ma cage?

UN VOYAGEUR

Hé! postillon!

UNE VOYAGEUSE

Postillon!

UN VOYAGEUR

Hé! postillon!

UNE VOYAGEUSE

Postillon!

UN VOYAGEUR

Ma malle!

UNE VOYAGEUSE

Mon panier!

LES HOMMES

Postillon!

LES FEMMES

Postillon!

LES POSTILLONS

Dans un moment!
Dans un moment!

TOUS

Donnez à chacun son bagage!

LES POSTILLONS

Moins de tapage!

TOUS

Voyons, voyons!

LES POSTILLONS

Non! Non! Non! Non!

VOYAGEURS

Dieux! quel tracas et quel tourment
Quand if faut monter en voiture!
Ah! je le jure,
On ferait bien de faire avant son testament!

POSTILLONS ET BOURGEOIS

Ah! c'est à se damner vraiment!
Chacun gémit et murmure!
Rien qu'en montant dans la voiture
Et recommence en descendant!

BOURGEOIS

Ah! c'est à se damner vraiment,
Chacun gémit!
Rien qu'en montant on descendant
Dieux! Quel tourment!

VOYAGEURS
(*poursuivant les Postillons*)

Je suis le premier!

POSTILLONS
(*brusquement*)

Le dernier!

BOURGEOIS
(*imitant les Postillons*)

Le dernier!

VOYAGEURS

Je suis le premier!

POSTILLONS ET BOURGEOIS

Non!

(*Manon qui vient de sortir de la foule considère tout ce tohu-bohu avec étonnement.*)

LESCAUT

Eh! j'imagine que cette belle enfant, c'est Manon! ma cousine! (*à Manon.*) Je suis Lescaut!

MANON

You! My cousin! Give me a kiss!

LESCAUT

Happy to oblige! Yes, indeed!
By heaven, she really is a beauty!
She is a credit to our family.

MANON (*embarrassed*)

Ah, my cousin, please excuse me.

LESCAUT (*aside*)

She is charming.

MANON

(*almost in tears from excitement*)

I've seen so much that amazes me,
I've seen so much that it dazes me.
All is so fair, all is so new,
Pardon the foolish things I do!
If I do something that you may
   deplore,
I've never been away from home before.

As soon as the coach had started
A marvellous world began to unfold,
Pretty towns, rolling fields and
   woodlands,
And all the travellers, young and old!
Ah, cousin, pardon me once more,
I've never been away from home before.

Everything was smiling and glowing,
The trees that blossomed on our way!
And I forgot where I was going,
The convent where I am to stay,
Where I must go this very day.
It all was so strange, so delightful . . .
You must not laugh! It is not nice!
Sometimes I thought that I was flying
And that I was in Paradise.

Then a sudden feeling of sadness
Made me cry. Never ask me why!
But all at once, a moment after
How I laughed! Never ask me why!
It's all so new, you must forgive
The foolish things I do.
I've seen so much that amazes me,
I've seen so much that it dazes me.
If I do something that you may
   deplore,
I've never been away from home
   before.

(*Further commotion. The travellers,
preceded by the Post-boys, swarm
back into the courtyard. A bell
sounds the warning that the coach
is to leave.*)

POST-BOYS (*to travellers*)

Come on. We're leaving.

TRAVELLERS (*recoiling at the thought*)

It's time to go?

POST-BOYS

Move on! Get in!
The other coach is waiting.

TRAVELLERS

To go? How so?
How very aggravating!
(*A near riot as the passengers reclaim
their luggage.*)

POST-BOYS

Come on!

TRAVELLERS

But my box! But my birds! My valise!

POST-BOYS

We're leaving! Come on!

ALL

Oh, not yet, oh, not yet!
We've been swindled!
(*The crowd goes out, leaving Lescaut
and Manon together.*)

LESCAUT (*going out*)

You stay here and wait. I will get your
baggage.

VILLAGERS

This we must know!
Ah, yes! Now we must go!
(*The villagers go out. Manon alone.*)
(*Guillot appears on the balcony of the
pavilion.*)

GUILLOT

That cursed innkeeper! It looks as if
   we're not going to have any wine!
(*seeing Manon*)
Heaven! What do I see! (*to Manon*)
Mademoiselle! (*aside*) What's happen-
   ing to my mind? This is amazing!

MANON (*aside*)

What a funny man!

GUILLOT

Mademoiselle, listen to me. My name is
   Guillot Morfontaine. I have lots of
   money and I'd give a lot to hear you
   say one loving word. That's all *I*
   have to say. What have *you* to say?

MANON

That I ought to be angry, but I'd
rather laugh.
(*Manon bursts out laughing, joined by
Brétigny, Poussette, Javotte and Rosette, who have come out on the balcony.*)

MANON

Vous mon cousin! Embrassez moi!

LESCAUT

Mais très volontiers, sur ma foi!
Morbleu! c'est une belle fille
Qui fait honneur à la famille!

MANON (*avec embarras*)

Ah! mon cousin, excusez moi!

LESCAUT (*à part*)

Elle est charmante!

MANON (*avec émotion*)

Je suis encor tout étourdie,
Je suis encor tout engourdie,
Ah! mon cousin! Excusez moi!
Excusez un moment d'émoi.
Je suis encor tout étourdie.

Pardonnez à mon bavardage,
J'en suis à mon premier voyage!

Le coche s'éloignait à peine,
Que j'admirais de tous mes yeux,
Les hameaux, les grands bois, la plai-

Les voyageurs jeunes et vieux!
Ah! mon cousin, excusez moi!
C'est mon premier voyage!
Je regardais fuir, curieuse,
Les arbres frissonnant au vent!
Et j'oubliais, toute joyeuse,
Que je partais pour le couvent!
Devant tant de choses nouvelles,
Ne riez pas, si je vous dis
Que je croyais avoir des ailes,
Et m'envoler au paradis!

Puis, j'eus un moment de tristesse,
Je pleurais, je ne sais pas quoi,
L'instant d'après, je le confesse,
Je riais mais sans savoir pourquoi!
Je suis encor tout étourdie,
Je suis encor tout engourdie!
Pardonnez à mon bavardage,
J'en suis à mon premier voyage!

LES POSTILLONS

Partez! On sonne!

VOYAGEURS

Comment? Partir!

LES POSTILLONS (*aux voyageurs*)

Allons! sortez! voici l'autre voiture!

VOYAGEUSES

Comment! partir! quelle mésaventure!

LES POSTILLONS

Partez!

UN VOYAGEURS

Mon carton! Mes oiseaux! Mon paquet!

LES POSTILLONS

Partez! On sonne!

VOYAGEURS

Mon chapeau!
On nous rançonne!
(*La cloche sonne.*)
(*La scène se vide peu à peu, la foule s'éloigne, laissant ensemble Lescaut et Manon.*)

LESCAUT

Attendez-moi, soyez bien sage.
Je vais chercher votre bagage!

BOURGEOIS

Il faut tout voir!
Pour nous c'est un devoir!
(*Entre Guillot sur le balcon.*)

GUILLOT

Hôtelier de malheur! Il est donc entendu que nous n'aurons jamais de vin! . . .
(*apercevant Manon*)
Ciel! qu'ai-je-vu? (*Il descend.*)
Mademoiselle! . . . hem! . . . hem! . . .
Mademoiselle . . .
(*à part*)
Ce qui se passe en ma cervelle est inouï!

MANON (*à part, en riant*)

Cet homme est fort drôle, ma foi!

GUILLOT

Mademoiselle, écoutez-moi!
On me nomme Guillot, Guillot de Morfontaine;
De louis d'or ma caisse est pleine,
Et j'en donnerais beaucoup pour
Obtenir de vous un seul mot d'amour.
J'ai fini, qu'avez-vous à dire?

MANON

Que je me fâcherais si je n'aimais mieux rire.
(*Son rire est répété par Brètigny, Javotte, Poussette et Rosette qui viennent d'arriver sur le balcon.*)

BRÉTIGNY

Well, Guillot, what are you doing?
We're waiting for you.

GUILLOT

To the devil with all fools!

POUSSETTE

Aren't you ashamed, at your age?

JAVOTTE, ROSETTE

At your age!

BRÉTIGNY

This time the fool has happened to
discover a treasure. There never was
such a sweet smile to light such a
lovely face.

POUSSETTE, JAVOTTE, ROSETTE
(laughing at Guillot)

Come away, Guillot, come away!
One misstep and down you will go!
One misstep, Guillot, and down you
go!
Come away, or you may
Live to rue the day!

BRÉTIGNY

Come on, Guillot, let her alone.
Come back here! They're calling you.

GUILLOT

All right, I'll come in a moment.
(to Manon) My sweet, just a word . . .

BRÉTIGNY

Guillot, let her alone . . .

GUILLOT (in a low voice, to Manon)

I will send my coachman here.
When he comes, my pretty dear,
You'll know my carriage is at hand,
And after that . . . you understand!
(Lescaut enters.)

LESCAUT (brusquely, to Guillot)

What's going on!

GUILLOT (stammering)

Monsieur!

LESCAUT

Monsieur! You were saying—

GUILLOT

Monsieur, I didn't say a word!
(He retreats to the pavilion.)

POUSSETTE, JAVOTTE,
ROSETTE, BRÉTIGNY

Come away, Guillot, etc.
(Laughing, they follow into the pavilion.)

LESCAUT (to Manon, seriously)

He spoke to you, Manon?

MANON

It really wasn't my fault.

LESCAUT

I know that.
I think too well of you, my dear,
To question what you may do.
(The two guardsmen return.)

FIRST GUARDSMAN

Lescaut, it's time to go.

SECOND GUARDSMAN

The cards and dice are waiting for you.

LESCAUT

I'll come. But before the cards and dice,
I must stay and give my young cousin
Some words of wisdom and fatherly
advice.

THE TWO GUARDSMEN (respectfully)

We must hear these words of wisdom.

LESCAUT (to Manon)

Look me in the eye, cousin dear!
I find that I must go and leave you
here.
My two friends and I must discuss
A certain matter that concerns only us.
You wait here for me. Don't go 'way.
I won't be long.
Be good, my child. Be quite genteel.
Do not forget our family name;
I must see that it is free from shame.
Protect our family name!
And if a man should come this way
With improper suggestions,
Just be careful and turn away,
Don't answer any foolish questions!
Tell him no, at least for a while,
Don't even smile!
Be good, my child. Be quite genteel.
Do not forget our family name;
I must see that it is free from shame,
Protect our family name!
(to the Guardsmen)
And now it's time for us to go and see
If Lady Luck will smile on you or me.
(As he is leaving, he turns back to
Manon.)
Be good, my child. Be quite genteel!

MANON

I shall stay here . . . since I must.
I will not even think.
I'll forget all the dreams and the long-
ings
That try to lead my heart astray.
Farewell to dreams!
(She glances toward the pavilion, where
she sees Poussette, Javotte and Ros-
ette.)

BRÉTIGNY
Eh bien, Guillot, que faites-vous?
Nous vous attendons!

GUILLOT
Au diable les fous!

POUSSETTE
N'avez-vous pas honte? . . . à votre
âge!

JAVOTTE, ROSETTE
. . . à votre âge!

BRÉTIGNY
Cette fois-ci, le drôle a par hasard
Découvert un trésor. Jamais plus doux
regard
N'illumina plus gracieux visage.

LES TROIS FEMMES
Revenez, Guillot, revenez!
Dieu sait où vous mène un faux pas,
Cher ami Guillot n'en faites pas!

BRÉTIGNY
Allons, Guillot, laissez Mademoiselle,
Et revenez, l'on vous appelle!

GUILLOT
Oui, je reviens dans un moment.
(à Manon)
Ma mignonne, un mot seulement!

BRÉTIGNY
Guillot, laissez Mademoiselle!

GUILLOT (bas, à Manon)
De ma part, tout à l'heure, un postillon
viendra . . .
Quand vous l'apercevrez, cela signi-
fiera
Qu'une voiture attend, que vous pou-
vez la prendre,
Et qu'après . . . vous devez com-
prendre . . .
(Lescaut vient de rentrer.)

LESCAUT
Plaît-il, Monsieur!

GUILLOT (épouvanté)
Monsieur?

LESCAUT
Eh bien!
Vous disiez . . .

GUILLOT
Je ne disais rien!
(Il se retire.)

BRÉTIGNY ET LES FEMMES
Revenez, Guillot, revenez, etc.
(Ils rentrent tous en riant le pavillon.)

LESCAUT (à Manon)
Il vous parlait, Manon?

MANON
Ce n'était pas ma faute.

LESCAUT
Certes! et j'ai de vous opinion trop
haute
Pour me fâcher.

PREMIER GARDE
Eh bien, tu ne viens pas?

DEUXIÈME GARDE
Les cartes et les dés nous attendent
là-bas!

LESCAUT
Je viens, mais à cette jeunesse
Permettez d'abord que j'adresse
Quelques conseils tout remplis de sa-
gesse!

LES GARDES (résignés)
Écoutons la sagesse.

LESCAUT (à Manon)
Regardez-moi bien dans les yeux!
Je vais tout près à la caserne,
Discuter avec ces messieurs
De certain point qui les concerne.
Attendez-moi donc un instant,
Un seul moment.

Ne bronchez pas, soyez gentille,
Et n'oubliez pas, mon cher coeur,
Que je suis gardien de l'honneur
De la famille!

Si par hasard, quelque imprudent
Vous tenait un propos frivole,
Dans la crainte d'un accident,
Ne dites pas une parole.
Priez-le d'attendre un instant,
Un seul moment.

Ne bronchez pas, soyez gentille
Et n'oubliez pas, mon cher coeur,
Que je suis gardien de l'honneur
De la famille!
(aux Gardes)
Et maintenant, voyons à qui de nous
La déesse du jeu va faire les yeux
doux!
(à Manon)
Ne bronchez pas, soyez gentille!

MANON
Restons ici, puisqu'il le faut!
Attendons sans penser! Evitons ces
folies!
Ces projets qui mettaient ma raison
en défaut!
Ne rêvons plus!
(Manon machinalement porte les yeux
sur le pavillon dans lequel sont enfer-
mées Poussette, Javotte, Rosette.)

Those other women are so lovely,
And the youngest is wearing a necklace
   of gold!
Ah, they must be ever so wealthy.
See how they've dressed their lovely
   hair!
Oh, that I were so charming and so
   fair!

Ah no, Manon, forget your dreaming,
It's no use to dream any more.
Leave all these thoughts of worldly
   beauty,
Leave them all at the convent door.

Ah no, Manon, it would not do.
Dreaming is not for you.
But what of them! They have beauty
   and leisure
For them life is always gay.
If I could only live that way
And be like them, and live for pleas-
   ure!

Ah no, Manon, forget your dreaming,
It's no use to dream any more.
Ah no, Manon, it would not do.
Dreaming is not for you.
(*Des Grieux enters without seeing
   Manon.*)

MANON

Who's that? Quick, back to my place!

DES GRIEUX (*to himself*)

I should be starting on my way.
It is strange. Somehow I want to stay.
I know that tomorrow night
I shall be with my father.
I can see him smiling
And my heart never led me wrong.
He will call, then he'll take me in his
   arms once more.
(*Des Grieux has turned toward
   Manon.*)

Oh heaven! Am I dreaming? Do I see
   a vision?
What moves my heart so deeply? I feel
   that my life
Is ending or beginning! It seems as if
   an iron hand
Compels me, in spite of myself,
To change my way, to go and stand
   before her.
          (*to Manon*)
Mademoiselle . . .

MANON

Sir?

DES GRIEUX

Forgive me. . . . I do not know. . . . I
obey. I am no longer my own master.
I know that this is the first time
I have seen you, yet my heart seems
to recognize you. And I must know
your name. . . .

MANON

You may call me Manon.

DES GRIEUX

Manon!

MANON (*aside*)

He has a gentle smile,
What a pleasure to hear him speaking!

DES GRIEUX

But I speak like a fool, my words stum-
ble and fall.

MANON

Don't condemn your dear words,
They have charmed my heart and my
   ears love to hear them.
How I wish I knew how to match
   them
With a charming reply!

DES GRIEUX

You are enchanting, I cannot resist
you!
Manon, Manon, you are the mistress of
my heart!

MANON

Charming words.

DES GRIEUX

O Manon!

MANON

What is this enchantment in my heart!

DES GRIEUX

Ah, tell me more!

MANON

I'm the daughter of simple people.
You must not think me wicked
But my family accuse me
Of loving pleasure and the joys of the
   world,
So they're sending me off to a convent.
Now you know the story of Manon
   Lescaut.

DES GRIEUX

No! I will not believe
That such a thing must be!
That so much beauty, so much charm
Must be wasted and hidden away in
   a tomb!

Combien ces femmes sont jolies!
La plus jeune portait un collier de
    grains d'or!
Ah! comme ces riches toilettes
Et ces parures si coquettes
Les rendaient plus belles encor!

Voyons, Manon, plus de chimères,
Où va ton esprit en rêvant?
Laisse ces désirs éphémères
A la porte de ton couvent!
Et cependant, pour mon âme ravie
En elles tout est séduisant!
Combien ce doit être amusant
De s'amuser toute une vie! . . .
Voyons, Manon, plus de chimères . . .
Où va ton esprit en rêvant?
Voyons, Manon, voyons Manon,
Plus de désirs, plus de chimères!

(*apercevant Des Grieux*)

Quelqu'un! Vite, à mon banc de pierre!

DES GRIEUX (*sans la voir*)

J'ai marqué l'heure du départ,
J'hésitais, chose singulière!
Enfin, demain soir ou plus tard
J'embrasserai mon père! . . . Oui, je le
    vois sourire,
Et mon coeur ne me trompe pas!
Je le vois, il m'appelle
Et je lui tends les bras!

(*Involontairement Des Grieux s'est
tourné vers Manon.*)

O ciel! Est-ce un rêve? Est-ce la folie?
D' où vient ce que j'éprouve? On dirait
    que ma vie
Va finir ou commence!, Il semble
    qu'une main
De fer me mène en un autre chemin
Et malgré moi m'entraîne devant
    elle! . . .

(*à Manon*)

Mademoiselle . . .

MANON

Eh quoi?

DES GRIEUX

Pardonnez-moi!
Je ne sais . . . j'obéis . . . je ne suis plus
    mon maître.
Je vous vois,
J'en suis sûr, pour la première fois
Et mon coeur cependant vient de vous
    reconnaître!
Et je sais votre nom . . .

MANON

On m'appelle Manon.

DES GRIEUX

Manon!

MANON (*à part*)

Que son regard est tendre!
Et que j'ai de plaisir à l'entendre!

DES GRIEUX

Ces paroles d'un fou, veuillez les par-
    donner!

MANON

Comment les condamner!
Elles charment le coeur en charmant
    les oreilles!
J'en voudrais savoir de pareilles
Pour vous les répéter!

DES GRIEUX

Enchanteresse!
Au charme vainqueur!
Manon! Vous êtes la maîtresse
De mon coeur!

MANON

Mots charmants!

DES GRIEUX

O Manon!

MANON

Enivrantes fièvres du bonheur!

DES GRIEUX

Ah! parlez-moi!

MANON

Je ne suis qu'une pauvre fille.
Je ne suis pas mauvaise, mais souvent
On m'accuse dans ma famille
D'aimer trop le plaisir. On me met au
    couvent
Tout à l'heure. Et c'est là l'histoire
De Manon Lescaut!

DES GRIEUX

Non! Je ne veux croire
A cette cruauté!
Que tant de charmes et de beauté
Soient voués à jamais à la tombe
    vivante!

MANON

It is the will of heaven itself
And I must obey.
What else is there to do
Since there's no other way!

DES GRIEUX

No! Beautiful Manon, you shall not
lose your freedom.

MANON

How so?

DES GRIEUX

You must rely on me,
The Chevalier Des Grieux.

MANON

Ah, you promise me much more than
life itself.

DES GRIEUX

Manon, you shall not leave me now!
Though you and I must search through
all the world,
I'll find a place where the world will
not find us
And carry you there in my arms.

MANON

You are my life and soul,
My heart is yours forever, all my heart.

DES GRIEUX

You are enchanting!
Manon, Manon, you are the mistress
of my heart.
(Manon sees the Post-boy whom Guillot
has sent to fetch her. She considers
a moment, and then smiles.)

MANON

I have a plan that will help us to get
away.
There is a carriage which belongs to a
noble lord.
He's been making eyes at Manon. Let's
get even!

DES GRIEUX

What do you mean?

MANON

Let us take it, you and I.

DES GRIEUX

Good! (to the Post-boy) Go and wait!
(The Post-boy leaves.)

MANON (wavering)

O dear! Do you think we ought to?

DES GRIEUX

Yes, Manon! Heaven has brought us
together.
Come to Paris with me!

MANON

You and I!

DES GRIEUX

You and I . . . We will be all alone.

MANON

In Paris!

DES GRIEUX

And our love shall make us one!

MANON

In Paris!

DES GRIEUX

You together with me.

BOTH

In the joy of the days to be!

DES GRIEUX

And my name shall become your own—
Ah, forgive me!

MANON

You must know that all I desire
Is to be yours and be with you.
And yet, perhaps, it's wrong!
(laughter from the pavilion)
O, I forgot about them!

DES GRIEUX

What's wrong?

MANON

Nothing. . . . Those beautiful women.

THE THREE WOMEN

Come away, Guillot, etc.

LESCAUT (off-stage, somewhat drunk)

You'll repay me tonight at the wine-
shop.

DES GRIEUX

Ah!

MANON

It's my cousin, Lescaut.

DES GRIEUX

Come! Come on!

POUSSETTE, JAVOTTE, ROSETTE
(offstage)

Come away, Guillot, come away, come
away!

MANON (to herself)

Ah! If only I could be that way
And be like them and live for pleasure!

MANON

Mais c'est, hélas! . . . la volonté
Du ciel dont je suis la servante,
Puisqu'un malheur si grand ne peut
être évité!

DES GRIEUX

Non! Votre liberté ne sera pas ravie!

MANON

Comment?

DES GRIEUX

Au chevalier Des Grieux vous pouvez
vous fier!

MANON

Je vous devrai plus que la vie!

DES GRIEUX

Ah, Manon! Vous ne partirez pas!
Dussé-je aller chercher au bout du
monde
Une retraite inconnue et profonde
Et vous y porter dans mes bras!

MANON

A vous ma vie et mon âme!
A vous toute ma vie à jamais!

DES GRIEUX

Enchanteresse!
Manon, vous êtes la maîtresse de mon
coeur!
(*Le postillon à qui Guillot a dit pré-
cedèmment de se tenir aux ordres de
Manon paraît dans le fond, Manon
le regarde, réfléchit et sourit.*)

MANON

Par aventure,
Peut-être avons-nous mieux:
Une voiture!
La chaise d'un seigneur! Il faisait
les doux yeux
A Manon. Vengez-vous!

DES GRIEUX

Mais comment?

MANON

Tous les deux, prenons-là!

DES GRIEUX (*au postillon*)

Soit, partons!
(*Le postillon se retire.*)

MANON

Eh quoi, partir ensemble?

DES GRIEUX

Oui, Manon! Le ciel nous rassemble!
Nous vivrons à Paris.

MANON

Tous les deux!

DES GRIEUX

Tous les deux, et nos coeurs amoureux.

MANON

A Paris!

DES GRIEUX

L'un à l'autre enchaînés.

MANON

A Paris!

DES GRIEUX

Pour jamais réunis.

MANON, DES GRIEUX

Nous n'aurons que des jours bénis!

DES GRIEUX

Et mon nom deviendra le vôtre!
Ah! pardon!

MANON

Dans mes yeux vous devez bien voir
Que je ne puis vous en vouloir;
Et cependant, c'est mal! . . .
(*Eclats de rire dans le pavillon*)
Ce sont elles!

DES GRIEUX

Qu'avez-vous?

MANON

Rien! ces femmes si belles!

LES TROIS FEMMES

Revenez donc, Guillot, revenez,
revenez!

LESCAUT (*au dehors, aviné*)

Ce soir, vous rendrez tout au cabaret
voisin!

DES GRIEUX

Là? . . .

MANON

C'est la voix de mon cousin!

DES GRIEUX

Viens! Partons!
(*Des Grieux l'entraine et Manon le
suit tout en regardant le pavillon où
sont Javotte, Poussette, etc.*)

POUSSETTE, JAVOTTE, ROSETTE
(*au dehors*)

Revenez, Guillot, revenez, revenez!

MANON (*à part*)

Combien ce doit être amusant
De s'amuser toute une vie!

MANON AND DES GRIEUX
Ah—we go!
(*They run away together.*)

LESCAUT (*enters, drunk*)
Not a sou! But how I love to play.
Hey, Manon! What! She's disappeared!
Hola! Hola!
GUILLOT (*coming softly down the steps*)
I must see her once again.

LESCAUT
Ah, it's you! The noble lord!

GUILLOT (*drawing back*)
What?

LESCAUT
You have abducted Manon. Give her
back!

GUILLOT (*terrified*)
Not so loud.

LESCAUT (*louder*)
Give her to me!
(*The villagers and the Innkeeper enter,
laughing at Guillot and Lescaut.*)

LESCAUT
Come on! Give her to me!

GUILLOT
Can you not see
How you are stirring up the people?

LESCAUT
Ah, bah! What's that to me!
(*to the crowd*)
He has stained our good name.
(*to Guillot*)
That girl is much too fine
For such a lout as you!

GUILLOT (*frightened*)
O what a scandal!

INNKEEPER AND VILLAGERS
Come on! You must explain!

GUILLOT
Please! Do let us be calm.
Let us be calm, let's keep our tempers!

LESCAUT (*more loudly*)
You speak up without any more delay.
I want Manon!

INNKEEPER
Oh, that young girl?
She went away with a fine young man.
She is gone!

GUILLOT
O Lord!

CHORUS
She went away.

LESCAUT
But what about our family name!

INNKEEPER
And in the coach that belongs to
Monsieur. . .

CHORUS
And in the coach that belongs to
Monsieur!

GUILLOT
No! Let me go, let go, let go!

LESCAUT
You wretch!

CHORUS (*laughing*)
This is a charming situation!

LESCAUT
No! I must avenge our honor!

CHORUS
This is a very sad affair!

BRÉTIGNY
(*coming from the pavilion with the
women*)
What now! Poor old Guillot!
So your lady has left you!

VILLAGERS
That such a gay seducer
Should have to suffer such a fate!

GUILLOT
You all be quiet! I will have my
revenge
Upon that ungrateful female and on
this drunken fool.

ALL (*without Lescaut*)
Ha ha! Ha ha!
A funny situation!
Oh, how very, very sad!

LESCAUT
Manon, Manon, I'll get you back some
day!
(*to Guillot*) And you, my friend, will
have to pay!

MANON, DES GRIEUX
Ah—partons!
(*Ils partent.*)

LESCAUT (*gris*)
Plus un sou!
Le tour est très plaisant,
Hé!. . . Manon!. . . Quoi! Disparue!
Holà!

GUILLOT
(*descendant doucement le balcon*)
Je veux la retrouver!

LESCAUT
Ah! c'est vous, le gros homme!

GUILLOT
Hein?

LESCAUT
Vous avez pris Manon, vous rendez-
la!

GUILLOT (*terrifié*)
Taisez-vous!

LESCAUT (*criant plus fort*)
Rendez-la-moi!
(*Les Bourgeois et L'Hôtelier arrivent
et se montrent en riant les deux
personnages.*)

LESCAUT
Allons! Rendez-la-moi!

GUILLOT (*bas*)
Regardez donc comme
Vous attirez la foule!

LESCAUT
Ah, bah! ça m'est égal!
(*aux Bourgeois*)
Il a pris notre honneur!
(*à Guillot*)
C'est un trop beau régal
Pour ton vilain museau!

GUILLOT
Quelle aventure!

L'HOTELIER ET LE CHOEUR
Voyons, expliquez-vous!

GUILLOT
Soit! Mais très doucement,
Très doucement et sans injure.

LESCAUT
Répondez catégoriquement:
Je veux Manon!

L'HOTELIER
Quoi! Cette jeune fille?
Elle est partie avec un jeune homme!
Écoutez!

GUILLOT
Ô ciel!

CHOEUR
Elle est partie!

LESCAUT
Mais c'est l'honneur de la famille!

L'HOTELIER
Dans la voiture de Monsieur!

CHOEUR
Dans la voiture de Monsieur!

GUILLOT
Non! Arrêtez! Lâchez! Lâchez!

LESCAUT
Gredin!

CHOEUR
Ah! Ah! La drôle de figure!

LESCAUT
Non! il faut que je châtie!

CHOEUR
Vit-on jamais pareil malheur!

BRÉTIGNY
(*sortant du pavillon avec les femmes*)
Eh! quoi! pauvre Guillot,
Votre belle est partie!

BOURGEOIS
Quelle mésaventure
Pour un aussi grand séducteur!

GUILLOT
Taisez-vous tous! Je veux être vengé
Et de cette perfide et de cet enragé!

TOUS (*sauf Lescaut*)
Ah! Ah! Ah! Ah!
La drôle de figure!
Ah, quel malheur!

LESCAUT
Morbleu! Manon! ah, vous me rever-
rez!
Et vous, petit, vous le paierez!

ACT TWO

The apartment of Des Grieux and Manon in the Rue Vivienne in Paris. There is an entrance door at right, a door at left, a small writing table, a table near the fire place. The furniture is simple. At the rear there is a window opening on the street.

(*Des Grieux sits at the writing desk. Manon comes quietly behind him trying to read what he is writing.*)

DES GRIEUX

(*as he stops writing, smiling but with a touch of reproach*)
Manon!

MANON (*gaily*)
Tell me, my dear, are you afraid
To have my cheek so close to yours?

DES GRIEUX
My impulsive Manon!

MANON
Now I can see over your shoulder.
It makes me smile, seeing you write my name.

DES GRIEUX
I am writing to my father, and I wonder
Whether these words, which I write from my heart,
Will annoy him.

MANON
Are you afraid?

DES GRIEUX
Yes, Manon, I'm afraid.

MANON
My dear, let us read it together.

DES GRIEUX
Yes, come and see,
Manon, read it with me!

MANON (*reading*)
"Her name is Manon. Yesterday she was sixteen.
In her all virtues meet, she has youth, she has beauty and grace.
There was never a voice so sweet,
There was never a face so loving and tender"...

DES GRIEUX (*repeating*)
There was never a face so loving and tender . . .

MANON (*She stops reading.*)
Is it true? I didn't know.
But I know that you love me well.

DES GRIEUX
Love you well? Manon, I adore you!

MANON (*freeing herself*)
Come, come! Let's read the letter!

DES GRIEUX (*reading*)
"Like the birds in the spring that follow the sun,
Her young soul awakes to life, her young heart always opens to beauty.
Her lips smile like the April flowers
When the perfumed breezes gently caress them."

MANON (*repeating*)
When the perfumed breezes gently caress them.
(*thoughtfully*)
Isn't it enough that we love each other?

DES GRIEUX
No. I want you to be my wife.

MANON
You really do?

DES GRIEUX
I want it with all my soul!

MANON
Then kiss me! Now send the letter!

DES GRIEUX
Yes, I'll take it right away.
(*He stops near the door.*)
Here are some flowers. Where did this bouquet come from, Manon?

MANON (*with animation*)
I don't know.

DES GRIEUX
What do you mean, you don't know?

MANON (*laughing*)
What a fine way to start a quarrel!

Someone threw them in the window.
They looked pretty so I kept them.
You're not really jealous?

DES GRIEUX (*tenderly*)
No, I can tell that your heart does not resist my love.

ACTE DEUXIÈME

L'appartement de Des Grieux et de Manon, rue Vivienne.—Porte d'entrée à droit, une porte à gauche. A gauche, premier plan, un petit bureau-secrétaire.—Une table près de la cheminée à droite.—Ameublement des plus simples.—Au fond, une fenêtre à petites vitres donnant sur la rue.

(Des Grieux est assis devant le bureau, Manon s'avance doucement derrière lui et cherche à lire ce qu'il écrit.)

DES GRIEUX

(s'arrêtant l'écrire et d'un ton de reproche; souriant)

Manon!

MANON *(gaîment)*

Avez-vous peur que mon visage frôle votre visage? . . .

DES GRIEUX

Indiscrète Manon!

MANON

Oui, je lisais sur votre épaule,
Et j'ai souri, voyant passer mon nom!

DES GRIEUX

J'écris à mon père et je tremble
Que cette lettre, où j'ai mis tout mon coeur,
Ne l'irrite . . .

MANON

Vous avez peur?

DES GRIEUX

Oui, Manon, j'ai très peur!

MANON

Eh bien! il faut relire ensemble.

DES GRIEUX

Oui, c'est cela, ensemble, relisons!

MANON *(lisant)*

"On l'appelle Manon; elle eut hier seize ans.
"En elle tout séduit, la beauté, la jeunesse,
"La grâce; nulle voix n'a de plus doux accents,
"Nul regard, plus de charme avec plus de tendresse."

DES GRIEUX *(répétant)*

Nul regard plus de charme avec plus de tendresse . . .

MANON *(s'arrêtant de lire)*

Est-ce vrai? Moi, je n'en sais rien;
Mais je sais que vous m'aimez bien!

DES GRIEUX

Vous aimer? Manon! Je t'adore!

MANON *(se dégageant)*

Allons, monsieur, lisons encore!

DES GRIEUX *(lisant)*

"Comme l'oiseau qui suit en tous lieux le printemps,
"Sa jeune âme à la vie est ouverte sans cesse;
"Sa lèvre en fleur sourit et parle
"Au zéphyr parfumé qui passe et la caresse!"

MANON *(répétant)*

Au zéphyr parfumé qui passe et la caresse!

(réfléchissant)

Il ne te suffit pas alors de nous aimer?

DES GRIEUX

Non! je veux que tu sois ma femme!

MANON

Tu le veux?

DES GRIEUX

Je le veux, et de toute mon âme!

MANON

Embrasse-moi donc, chevalier,
Et va porter ta lettre.

DES GRIEUX

Oui, je vais la porter!
(Il s'arrête et regarde un bouquet qui est placé sur la cheminée.)
Voilà des fleurs qui sont fort belles;
D'où te vient ce bouquet, Manon?

MANON *(vivement)*

Je ne sais pas.

DES GRIEUX

Comment, tu ne sais pas?

MANON *(riant)*

Beau motif de querelles! Par la fenêtre, on l'a lancé d'en bas.
Comme il était joli, je l'ai gardé. Je pense que tu n'es pas jaloux?

DES GRIEUX *(tendrement)*

Non, je puis te jurer que je n'ai de ton coeur aucune défiance.

MANON

You're right. My heart belongs to you.
(*loud noises outside*)

DES GRIEUX

What's going on out there?
(*Enter the maid, frightened.*)

THE MAID

There are two guardsmen out there.
They're very angry. One says he is a
relative of Madame.

MANON

Lescaut, it's Lescaut!

THE MAID (*aside to Manon*)

The other one . . . he is . . . we mustn't
speak too loud . . . the other one is
a man who is in love with you . . .
the tax commissioner who lives near
here . . .

MANON (*softly*)

Monsieur de Brétigny?

THE MAID

Monsieur de Brétigny.

DES GRIEUX

This is too much! I'll see to it myself.
(*As he approaches the door, it is
opened by Lescaut. Brétigny, in a
guardsman's uniform, is with him.*)

LESCAUT

The love-birds in their nest!
I have caught you at last!

BRÉTIGNY

Don't be too harsh, Lescaut!
They are young, and they're in love.

LESCAUT (*to Des Grieux*)

Do you think it was polite to treat me
like a fool, you young seducer?

DES GRIEUX

What's that! Mind what you say, my
friend!

LESCAUT (*ironically*)

Mind what I say?

DES GRIEUX (*calmly*)

Mind what you say!

LESCAUT

It is enough to drive a saint to drink!
I've come today to avenge the honor
of our family,
I've come to right a wrong,
To make the guilty pay,
And now you have the nerve to tell me
What I am to say!

BRÉTIGNY

Be calm!

LESCAUT

You thief!

BRÉTIGNY

Go slow!

DES GRIEUX

All right! I'll slice both your ears from
your head!

LESCAUT

(*to Brétigny, pretending not to understand*)
What did he say?

BRÉTIGNY (*laughing*)

He said he would cut your ears off.

LESCAUT

I do believe that he means to insult me!
Does he mean it?

BRÉTIGNY

I think he does.

LESCAUT

By death and by hell!

BRÉTIGNY

Do be calm, Lescaut! Come on!
Their remorse fills them with shame.
See! Both of them take the blame.
Don't be so angry! Do be calm!

DES GRIEUX

O Manon, do not be afraid: Rely on
me!
I am the one who is to blame.
Oh my dear love, you're trembling so!
I'll calm him down and take the blame.

LESCAUT

You thief! (*to Brétigny*) You hold me
back.
Rascal! You hold me back!
Or I'll do something I'll regret,
He'll learn a lesson that he won't for-
get.

MANON (*to Des Grieux*)

My dear, my dear, I'm so afraid,
I know so well that I'm to blame.
Stay close to me! His angry words put
me to shame.

BRÉTIGNY

Lescaut, you are going too far.
Why not explain why you are here?

LESCAUT

Yes, I'll make it clear.
(*to Des Grieux*)
Manon's my cousin, and I've come here
As polite as I can be . . .

MANON

Et tu fais bien! Ce coeur est à toi tout
 entier!
(*On entend un bruit de voix au dehors.*)

DES GRIEUX

Qui donc se permet un pareil tapage?
(*Entre la Servante effarée.*)

LA SERVANTE

Deux gardes du corps sont là qui font
 rage;
L'un se dit le parent de madame.

MANON

Lescaut! C'est Lescaut!

LA SERVANTE (*bas à Manon*)

L'autre c'est . . . ne parlons pas trop
 haut,
L'autre, c'est quelqu'un qui vous aime,
Ce fermier général qui loge près d'ici.

MANON (*bas*)

Monsieur de Brétigny? . . .

LA SERVANTE

Monsieur de Brétigny.

DES GRIEUX

Cela devient trop fort et je vais voir
 moi-même.
(*Au moment où il va s'élancer, la porte s'ouvre. Entrent Brétigny et Lescaut costumé en garde du corps.*)

LESCAUT

Enfin, les amoureux,
Je vous tiens tous les deux!

BRÉTIGNY

Soyez clément, Lescaut, songez à leur
 jeunesse!

LESCAUT

Vous m'avez, l'autre jour, brûlé la po-
 litesse, monsieur le drôle!

DES GRIEUX

Hé là! parlez plus doucement!

LESCAUT (*ironique*)

Plus doucement?

DES GRIEUX (*calme*)

Plus doucement!

LESCAUT

C'est à tomber froudroyé sur la place!
J'arrive pour venger l'honneur de notre race,
Je suis le redresseur, je suis le châti-
 ment,
Et c'est à moi qu'on dit de parler doucement!

BRÉTIGNY

Contiens-toi!

LESCAUT

Coquin!

BRÉTIGNY

Retiens-toi!

DES GRIEUX

C'est bien! Je vais vous couper les
 oreilles!

LESCAUT (*se reculant*)

Qu'est-ce qu'il dit?

BRÉTIGNY (*riant*)

Qu'il va vous couper les oreilles.

LESCAUT

Vit-on jamais insolences pareilles?
Il menace?

BRÉTIGNY

Ça m'en a l'air.

LESCAUT

Par la mort, par l'enfer!

BRÉTIGNY

Contiens-toi, Lescaut, allons!
Chacun d'eux est coupable.
Le remords les accable! Vois!
Contiens-toi, Lescaut, retiens-toi!

DES GRIEUX

O Manon, soyez sans effroi!
Seul de nous deux, je suis coupable,
Il bientôt sera plus traitable;
O Manon, comptez sur moi!

LESCAUT

Coquin!
Retenez-moi!
Je sais de quoi je suis capable,
Quand il faut punir un coupable!
Drôle! Retenez-moi! Retenez-moi!

MANON (*à Des Grieux*)

Ah! chevalier, je meurs d'effroi!
Je le sais bien, je suis coupable!
Son regard courroucé m'accable.
Ah! chevalier, veillez sur moi!

BRÉTIGNY

Lescaut, vous montrez trop de zèle!
Expliquez-vous plus posément.

LESCAUT

Soit, j'y consens.
(*à Des Grieux*)
Mademoiselle est ma cousine, et je
 venais très poliment . . .

DES GRIEUX

As you can be?

LESCAUT

As I can be,
I've been polite as I can be
To say this: "Monsieur, I do not seek
a quarrel,
Just answer yes or answer no!
Do you intend to marry Manon?"

BRÉTIGNY AND LESCAUT

For men like us
There is no need
To make a fuss,
When we can settle this discreetly!

BRÉTIGNY (laughing, to Des Grieux)

What more does your honor require?

DES GRIEUX (also laughing)

My anger has vanished completely,
Your frankness is all I desire.

(He shows the letter to Lescaut.)

I have written a note to my father.
Before I seal it for the mail,
I would be pleased if you would read
it.

LESCAUT (taking the letter)

That I will! It's getting so dark,
Come over here where we can see,
Let us stand by the window
Where it will be easy to read it.

(He goes to the window with Des
Grieux. Brétigny is near Manon.)

MANON (to Brétigny)

Coming like this and dressed up in
disguise! . . .

BRÉTIGNY

Aren't you pleased?

MANON

I am annoyed.
You must know that I truly love him.

BRÉTIGNY

But I only wanted to come and warn
you
That tonight they will come to take
Des Grieux away?

MANON

Tonight?
Des Grieux away?

BRÉTIGNY

By order of his father.

MANON

By order of his father!

BRÉTIGNY

Yes, tonight they will take him,
They will take him from here . . .

MANON (stepping away)

Ah, he must be warned right away!

BRÉTIGNY (stopping her)

If you prevent it,
Life will be hard for him, for you,
But if you let them come,
I'll see that your future, your fortune
Are all assured.

MANON

Don't speak so loud!

LESCAUT (reading the letter)

"Her name is Manon.
Yesterday she was sixteen.
In her all virtues meet". . . .
How these words touch my heart!

MANON (to Brétigny)

No! No! I can't.

DES GRIEUX

Ah, Lescaut, that's how much I love
her,
I say again that I adore her!

BRÉTIGNY

Manon, Manon, it's your hour of de-
cision
Calling you to be free!
Manon, Manon, because of your beauty
You shall be queen of all.

MANON

I'm filled with doubt, I'm so afraid,
And my heart must be breaking!

LESCAUT (to Des Grieux)

You'll marry her?

(reading)

"Like the birds in the spring". . .
That is poetry, that's love!
"Her young soul awakes to life". . .
That is poetry!
"Always opens to beauty". . .
That's love!

(to Des Grieux)

That is perfect! I could do no better.
Let me present my compliments to you!
(to Manon) My cousin! (to Des
Grieux) My cousin too!
My sincere felicitations!
Now take my hand. I really can't con-
demn you
For being so in love. My dears, bless-
ings on you both!
I'm weeping! Good luck!
(to Brétigny, with a change of tone)
Shall we go?

DES GRIEUX

Très poliment?

LESCAUT

Très poliment;
Oui, je venais très poliment
Dire: "Monsieur, sans vous chercher
    querelle,
Répondez: Oui, répondez: Non,
Voulez-vous épouser Manon?"

BRÉTIGNY ET LESCAUT

La chose est claire,
Entre lurons
Et bons garçons,
C'est ainsi qu'on traite une affaire!

BRÉTIGNY (à Des Grieux riant)

Eh bien, êtes-vous satisfait?

DES GRIEUX (de même)

Ma foi, je n'ai plus de colère,
Et votre franchise me plaît.

(montrant sa lettre a Lescaut)

Je venais d'écrire à mon père . . .
Avant qu'on y mette un cachet,
Vous lirez bien ceci, j'espère.

LESCAUT

Volontiers! Mais voici le soir!
Allons tous deux, pour y mieux voir,
Nous placer près de la fenêtre,
Et là nous lirons votre lettre.
(Il remont vers le fond avec Des
    Grieux. Brétigny se trouve près de
    Manon.)

MANON (à Brétigny)

Venir ici sous un déguisement!

BRÉTIGNY

Vous m'en voulez?

MANON

Certainement!
Vous savez que c'est lui que j'aime!

BRÉTIGNY

J'ai voulu vous avertir, moi-même,
Que ce soir de chez vous, on compte
    l'enlever.

MANON

Ce soir?

BRÉTIGNY

Par ordre de son père.

MANON

Par ordre de son père!

BRÉTIGNY

Oui, ce soir, d'ici même on viendra
    l'arracher.

MANON (faisant un pas)

Ah! je saurai bien empêcher.

BRÉTIGNY (l'arrêtant)

Prévenez-le, c'est la misère
Pour lui, pour vous; ne le prévenez
    pas,
Et c'est la fortune, au contraire,
Qui vous attend.

MANON

Parlez plus bas!

LESCAUT (lisant)

"On l'appelle Manon,
Elle eut hier seize ans....
"En elle tout séduit!" Que ces mots
    sont touchants!

MANON

Non, non! Jamais!

DES GRIEUX

Ah! Lescaut, c'est que je l'adore!
Laissez-moi vous le dire encore!

BRÉTIGNY

Manon, voici l'heure prochaine
De votre liberté!
Manon, bientôt vous serez reine,
Reine par la beauté!

MANON

Dans mon cœur quel délire!
Quel doute étrange et quel tourment!

LESCAUT

Vous l' épousez?
"Comme l'oiseau qui suit le prin-
    temps!"
Poèsie! Amour!
"Sa jeune âme à la vie est ouverte sans
    cesse."
O poésie! amour! . . .
            (à Des Grieux)
C'est parfait! On ne peut mieux dire,
Et je vous fais mon compliment!
Cousine, et vous cousin, je vous rends
    mon estime.
Prenez ma main, car ce serait un
    crime
De vous tenir rigueur; enfants, je vous
    bénis.
Les larmes . . . le bonheur!
            (changement de ton, à Brétigny)
Partons-nous?

BRÉTIGNY
Let us go!

LESCAUT AND BRÉTIGNY (*as they go*)
For men like us
There is no need
To make a fuss.
The thing is done, and very neatly!
(*They go out.*)

MANON (*to herself*)
What shall I do!

DES GRIEUX (*to himself*)
Soon may the sun of my happiness
Be rising and smiling on me!
(*The Maid enters.*)

MANON
What is it?

THE MAID
It's time for supper, Monsieur.

DES GRIEUX
So it is! And I haven't yet posted my
    letter.

MANON
Better do it now.

DES GRIEUX (*coming toward Manon*)
Manon!

MANON (*disturbed*)
Later on?

DES GRIEUX
I love you, I adore you. And you . . .
    do you love me?

MANON
Yes, my dear, I love you.

DES GRIEUX
Then you ought to promise me . . .

MANON
What?

DES GRIEUX
Nothing . . . nothing at all. I will go
and send the letter.
(*He goes out.*)

MANON (*very troubled*)
I must give him up for his own sake!
My poor chevalier!
Ah yes, I really love him.
How can I decide what to do?
No, no! I do not deserve such a love.
I still hear that voice that persuades
    me
Like a beckoning call:
"Manon, because of your beauty,

You shall be queen of them all."
I am weak and uncertain how to make
    up my mind . . .
Ah, even now, in spite of myself I'm
    weeping,
Weeping for dreams that could not last.
What's to come? Will the future give
    me
Moments like those that now have
    past?
(*Little by little she has come toward
    the table where the supper has been
    prepared.*)
Farewell, our friendly little table
Where we two would meet every day!
Farewell, our friendly little table
So small yet so dear and so gay!
How strange that such a little table
Bound us together in such a way!

Farewell, our friendly little table!
We drank from one dear glass together,
And when I tried to sip the wine
His lips would reach for mine.
Ah, my poor love, how well you loved
    me!
Farewell, our friendly little table,
Farewell!
(*She hears Des Grieux returning.*)
He's here! I must look pale!
I wonder if he'll see.
(*Des Grieux enters.*)

DES GRIEUX
Darling, at last we are alone together!
My dear, you're crying!

MANON
No!

DES GRIEUX
Your hand . . . it is trembling!

MANON (*trying to smile*)
The table is prepared.

DES GRIEUX
Ah, yes! My mind was astray.
Our new-found happiness may fly
Like a bird into the sky.
It must be cherished lest it fly away.
To the table!

MANON
To the table!

DES GRIEUX
In this dear moment all fear is
    forgotten,
We are here alone, you and I.
Ah, Manon! On my way
I lost myself in dreaming!

MANON (*aside, with bitterness*)
Alas, so much of life is dreaming!

BRÉTIGNY

Je vous suis!

LESCAUT ET BRÉTIGNY (*s'éloignant*)

La chose est claire!
Entre lurons
Et bons garçons,
C'est ainsi qu'on traite une affaire!
    (*Ils sortent.*)

MANON

Dans mon coeur quel tourment!

DES GRIEUX

Puis du bonheur où j' aspire
Le jour se lever souriant!
    (*Entre la Servante.*)

MANON

Que nous veut-on?

LA SERVANTE

C'est l'heure du souper, Monsieur.

DES GRIEUX

C'est vrai pourtant. Et je n'ai pas encore porté ma lettre!

MANON

Eh bien, va la porter.

DES GRIEUX
(*s'approchant de Manon*)

Manon!

MANON (*distraite*)

Après?

DES GRIEUX

Je t'aime, je t'adore! Et toi, dis,
m'aimes-tu?

MANON (*de même*)

Oui, mon cher chevalier . . .
Je t'aime.

DES GRIEUX

Tu devrais, en ce cas, me promettre . . .

MANON

Quoi?

DES GRIEUX

Rien du tout, je vais porter ma lettre!
    (*Il sort.*)

MANON (*très troublée*)

Allons! il le faut! Pour lui-même!
Mon pauvre chevalier! . . . Oh! oui,
    c'est lui que j'aime
Et pourtant j'hésite aujourd'hui!
Non! non! je ne suis plus digne de lui!
J'entends cette voix qui m'entraine
Contre ma volonté:
"Manon, tu seras reine,
Reine par la beauté!"
Je ne suis que faiblesse et que fragilité!
Ah! malgré moi je sens couler mes
    larmes
Devant ces rêves effacés!
L'avenir aura-t-il les charmes
De ces beaux jours déjà passés?
(*Peu à peu elle s'est approchée de la
    table toute servie.*)
Adieu, notre petite table
Qui nous réunit si souvent!
Adieu, notre petite table,
Si grande pour nous cependant!
On tient, c'est inimaginable,
Si peu de place en se serrant!
Un même verre était le nôtre,
Chacun de nous, quand il buvait
Y cherchait les lèvres de l'autre . . .
Ah! Pauvre ami, comme il m'aimait!
Adieu! Notre petite table!
Adieu!

C'est lui! Que ma pâleur ne me
    trahisse pas!

DES GRIEUX

Enfin, Manon, nous voilà seuls ensemble!
Quoi? des larmes?

MANON

Non!

DES GRIEUX

Si fait, ta main tremble.

MANON (*s'efforçant de sourire*)

Voici notre repas.

DES GRIEUX

C'est vrai! ma tête est folle!
Mais le bonheur est passager,
Et le ciel l'a fait si léger
Qu'on a toujours peur qu'il s'envole!
A table!

MANON

A table!

DES GRIEUX

Instant charmant où la crainte fait
    trêve,
Où nous sommes deux seulement!
Tiens, Manon, en marchant, je viens
    de faire un rêve.

MANON (*avec amertume, à part*)

Hélas! qui ne fait pas de rêve?

DES GRIEUX

When I close my eyes I seem to see
A house in a garden,
Just a humble dwelling
Fair and white beneath a tree.
And there I see smiling flowers,
The brook gently flows along,
Murmuring through the happy hours
As the birds sing their song.
It is heaven on earth! . . . Oh, no!
One thing only still is wanting,
For heaven cannot be heaven
Without my love Manon!

MANON (*softly*)

It's a dream, only a dream!

DES GRIEUX

No! That is our life together
If I have you, Oh, Manon!
(*Someone knocks at the door.*)

MANON

Oh God! Already!

DES GRIEUX

Who's there?
This is no time for interruptions . . .
(*He gets up.*)
I'll send this intruder away . . .
But I'll return.

MANON

Adieu!

DES GRIEUX (*surprised*)

But why?

MANON

(*embarrassed, suppressing her feelings*)
No! I want you here!

DES GRIEUX

But why?

MANON

Please do not open that door!
I want to stay in your arms!

DES GRIEUX (*tenderly freeing himself*)

My dear, let me go!

MANON

No!

DES GRIEUX

What's the trouble?

MANON

No!

DES GRIEUX

Come, come!

MANON

Do not go!

DES GRIEUX

Who can it be? It's rather strange.
I'll send him away as politely as I can.
When I return, we shall laugh together
at your foolish fancies.

(*He embraces her and goes out to open
the door. Sounds of a struggle are
heard. Manon runs to the window.
There are sounds of a carriage rum-
bling away.*)

MANON

My poor chevalier!

ACT THREE

SCENE I

*Cours la Reine, Paris. The promenade,
on a holiday. Among the tall trees
are the shops of toy-sellers, dress-
makers, tobacconists, restaurant-
keepers, peddlers, merchants, etc. At
the right, an open dance hall. The
curtain rises on a scene of promenaders, nobles and townspeople, while
the shopkeepers and peddlers cry
their wares.*

MODISTES

Dainty slippers! Lovely laces!
Buy your girl a scarf and veil!
Bonnets, bustles, collarettes!
Linen, silk and fine percale!

A PEDDLER

Tonics for every disease!

A WOMAN

Paint and powder for your faces,
Flowers, feathers, fine aigrettes!

THE PEDDLER

Tobacco that's certain to please!

BALLAD-SELLER

All the latest songs for sale!

A COOK

Everybody come and eat now!
I can promise you a treat now!

A GROUP OF PEDDLERS

Get your tickets for the lottery!
Ribbons, canes and fancy hats!
See my fine imported pottery!
Children's toys and balls and bats!

DES GRIEUX

En fermant les yeux, je vois
Là-bas une humble retraite,
Une maisonnette
Toute blanche au fond des bois!
Sous ses tranquilles ombrages
Les clairs et joyeux ruisseaux,
Où se mirent les feuillages,
Chantent avec les oiseaux!
C'est le paradis! Oh! non!
Tout est là triste et morose,
Car il y manque une chose:
Il y faut encor Manon!

MANON (*doucement*)

C'est un rêve, une folie!

DES GRIEUX

Non!
Non! Là sera notre vie,
Si tu le veux, ô Manon!
(*On entend frapper doucement à la
porte.*)

MANON

Oh ciel! déjà!

DES GRIEUX

Quelqu'un?
Il ne faut pas de trouble fête.
(*se levant*)
Je vais renvoyer l'importun,
Et je reviens!

MANON (*troublée*)

Adieu!

DES GRIEUX (*étonné*)

Comment?

MANON
(*avec embarras et émotion contenue*)
Non . . . Je ne veux pas! . . .

DES GRIEUX

Pourquoi?

MANON

Tu n'ouvriras pas cette porte!
Je veux rester dans tes bras! . . .

DES GRIEUX
(*se dégageant doucement*)
Enfant! Laisse-moi!

MANON

Non!

DES GRIEUX

Que t'importe!

MANON

Non!

DES GRIEUX

Allons!

MANON

Je ne veux pas.

DES GRIEUX

Quelque inconnu! C'est singulier!
Je le congédierai d'une façon polie.
Je reviens, nous rirons tous deux de
ta folie!
(*Il l'embrasse et sort. On entend un
bruit de lutte. Manon se lève et court
vers la fenêtre.—
Roulement de voiture.*)

MANON

Mon pauvre chevalier!

ACTE TROISIÈME.

PREMIER TABLEAU

*La promenade du Cours la Reine un
jour de fête populaire. A droite,
l'enseigne d'un bal. Entre les
grands arbres, des boutiques de
marchands de toutes sortes: modistes, marchands de jouets, saltim-
banques, marchands de chansons,
etc.*

LES MODISTES

Voyez mules à fleurettes!
Fichus et coqueluchons,
Bonnets, paniers, collerettes,
Gaze, linons et manchons!

UN MARCHAND

Elixir pour l'estomac!

UNE MARCHANDE

Rouge, mouches et manchettes!
Plumes et fines aigrettes!

LE MARCHAND

Poudre, râpes à tabac!

UN MARCHAND DE CHANSONS

Achetez-moi mes chansons!

UN CUISINIER

Il est temps qu'on se régale,
Ma cuisine est sans égale!

UN GROUPE DE MARCHANDS

Billets pour la loterie,
Rubans, cannes et chapeaux!
Bonbons et pâtisserie,
Jouets, balles et sabots!

GENERAL CHORUS

It's here at Cours la Reine
   That we drink and we sing,
And fill the glass again
   To toast our glorious King!

(*Poussette and Javotte come out of the dance hall. Soon afterwards, Rosette enters. Three young men, at a signal from the girls, run to meet them.*)

POUSSETTE AND JAVOTTE

What a charming place for walking!
   Ah, how lovely, ah, how dear!
Ah, how fine a place for talking,
   No one near to overhear!

POUSSETTE

That's understood.

JAVOTTE

You must take care!

ROSETTE

A word might give us all away.

POUSSETTE

That's understood!

JAVOTTE

My heart agrees to all you say.

POUSSETTE, JAVOTTE AND ROSETTE

But poor Guillot must never know!

(*Poussette and Javotte go back to the dance hall, Rosette disappears into the crowd.*)

(*Lescaut pushes his way through the crowd, pursued by the Peddlers who press their wares upon him.*)

PEDDLERS

Take this, Monsieur!
No, this Monsieur!
A splendid bargain!
Come and take your choice!

LESCAUT

My choice? But why?
I'll buy your whole supply!
Bring me some more!
I don't ask you the price!
These are for the lady I adore.
I will rely on your advice.
What's the use of hesitating
When I have three dice to play,
And I'll soon be on my way
To where my Lady Luck is waiting?

PEDDLERS

How cheap! How nice,
At twice the price!

LESCAUT

No, that's enough!

O, Rosalinda!
Were I to climb the heights of Pindus,
I could not praise you as I ought!
The queens who reign beyond the
   Indus,
And fair Armida and Clorinda,
What are they, beside you? Naught!
They're as naught!
O, my Rosalinda!
I'll climb the heights of Pindus
To sing your praises as I ought!

Choose? Choose? No, not I!
What's the use of hesitating
When I have three dice to play,
And I'll soon be on my way
To where my Lady Luck is waiting?
My dears, my darlings, come and see!
I have a pearl for every girl
Who has a little kiss for me!
(*He leaves, pursued by the Peddlers.*)
(*Poussette, Javotte and Rosette come out of the dance hall.*)

GUILLOT (*seeing them*)

Ah, there, Poussette!

POUSSETTE (*with a startled cry*)

Oh, heavens!

GUILLOT

My dear Javotte!

JAVOTTE (*crying out*)

Oh Lord!
(*Poussette and Javotte run away.*)

GUILLOT

And you, Rosette!

ROSETTE

Ah!
(*She runs away.*)

GUILLOT

By all that's holy! They've given me the slip! The little devils! And to think I brought all three of them, so that even if one or two got away, I could count on the other to be faithful! I swear, a woman is a wicked creature!

BRÉTIGNY

(*enters and overhears the last remark*)
You're quite right, Guillot, you're quite

CHOEUR GÉNÉRAL

C'est fête au Cours la Reine!
On y rit, on y boit,
Pendant une semaine,
A la santé du Roi!

(*Poussette et Javotte, puis Rosette par-
aissent dans la foule; trois petits
clercs les aperçoivant et, sur un signe
d'elles, courent à leur recontre.*)

POUSSETTE, JAVOTTE

La charmante promenade,
Ah! que ce séjour est doux!
Que c'est bon une escapade,
Loin des regards d'un jaloux!

POUSSETTE

C'est entendu!

JAVOTTE

Tenez-vous bien!

ROSETTE

Un mot pourrait me compromettre!

POUSSETTE

C'est entendu!

JAVOTTE

Mon coeur veut bien tout vous promettre!

POUSSETTE, JAVOTTE ET ROSETTE

Mais que Guillot n'en sache rien!

(*Poussette, Javotte et Rosette
s'éloignent.*)

MARCHANDS (*poursuivant Lescaut*)

Tenez, monsieur!
Prenez, monsieur!
Prenez! Choisissez!

LESCAUT

Choisir! Et pourquoi?
Donnez! donnez encore!
Ce soir j'achète tout!
C'est pour la beauté que j'adore,
Je m'en rapporte à votre goût!
A quoi bon l'économie
Quand on a trois dés en main,
Et que l'on sait le chemin
De l'hôtel de Transylvanie!

LES MARCHANDS

Tenez! Prenez!

LESCAUT

Assez! Assez!

O Rosalinde,
Il me faudrait gravir le Pinde,
Pour te chanter comme il convient!
Que sont les sultanes de l'Inde
Et les Armide et les Clorinde
Près de toi, que sont-elles? Rien,
Rien du tout, ô ma Rosalinde!

Choisir! Choisir! non, ma foi!
A quoi bon l'économie
Quand on a trois dés en main
Et que l'on sait le chemin
De l'hôtel de Transylvanie!
Approchez, ô belles! approchez!
J'offre un bijou pour deux baisers!

(*Il sort, poursuivi par les marchands.*)

(*Guillot, Poussette, Javotte, Rosette et
les Petits Clercs.*)

GUILLOT (*les apercevant*)

Bonjour, Poussette!

POUSSETTE (*avec un cri*)

Ah! ciel!

GUILLOT

Bonjour, Javotte!

JAVOTTE (*de même*)

Ah! Dieu!

GUILLOT

Bonjour, Rossette!

ROSETTE

Ah!

GUILLOT

Par la morbleu! Elles me plantent là.
Coquine! Péronnelle! Et j'en avais
pris trois . . . pourtant il me semblait
pouvoir compter, si l'une me trom-
pait, qu'une autre au moins serait
fidèle! La femme est, je l'avoue, un
méchant animal!

BRÉTIGNY (*entrant*)

Pas mal, Guillot, ce mot-là n'est pas

right. But you're not the first man to say so.

(*Guillot frowns fiercely.*)

Heavens! What a gloomy face! I'll bet that Javotte has been up to her tricks!

GUILLOT

Javotte? That's all over.

BRÉTIGNY

And Poussette?

GUILLOT

The same with Poussette!

BRÉTIGNY

Then you're a free man? (*making fun*) Guillot, promise you won't take Manon away from me?

GUILLOT

Take Manon from you?

BRÉTIGNY

No! Swear that you won't!

GUILLOT

Don't talk nonsense . . . By the way, speaking of Manon, I hear that she asked you to bring the Opera to perform for her at home, and you refused. Even when she begged with tears in her eyes, you said: NO!

BRÉTIGNY

Yes, you're right. That story is true.

GUILLOT

I see. . . . Excuse me if I leave you for a moment. I'll be back soon.

(*He goes out, humming to himself in glee.*)

Dig a dig a don!
I shall steal away your Manon!

(*The Peddlers and Promenaders return.*)

PEDDLERS AND TOWNSPEOPLE

(*staring at the gay Parisiennes*)

No wonder they're entrancing!
They spend their time romancing,
Pretty things to wear,
Life without a care!

(*Manon enters, with Brétigny and several young noblemen.*)

TOWNSMEN

Who is that lovely lady?
She must be at least a duchess!

TOWNSWOMEN

Oh, you must surely know her name!
That's Manon, the famous Manon!

BRÉTIGNY AND NOBLES

Most enchanting Manon!

MANON

You really find me so fair?

BRÉTIGNY AND NOBLES

You are lovely, alluring, delightful!

MANON

Is that so? Then I thank you!
In return, I feel it my duty
To permit you to worship
My charm and my beauty!

I go my triumphant way
With no other rivals remaining,
All the world adores me today,
As beauty's new queen I am reigning.

When my horses prance through the street
The crowd finds it somewhat alarming,
The nobles all kneel at my feet,
I have beauty, and life is charming.

So let all my life be gay,
I care not for what may after;
And if Manon should die some day
Then let me die, my friends,
In revelry and laughter.

THE OTHERS

Bravo, Manon!

MANON

Let us obey when love is calling,
Calling us to laugh and dance,
When beauty offers all her fleeting
hours of sweet romance.
Let there be no sorrowing and sighing,
Youth is the time to sing.
Come while your golden hours are flying,
Oh, come and taste the joy of Spring!

BRÉTIGNY AND NOBLES

Let there be no sorrowing and sighing,
Now is the time, bright hours are flying.

MANON

For sad to say, the truest lover
May forget his love some day.
So why delay and then discover
Youth has flown away?
(*to Brétigny*)
You wait for me here, there are things
I must buy,
And I may take some time in the choosing.

mal! Mais il n'est pas de vous!
(*Guillot le regarde avec fureur.*)
Dieu! quel sombre visage!
Dame Javotte, je le gage,
Vous aura fait des traits!

GUILLOT
Javotte, c'est fini!

BRÉTIGNY
Et Poussette?

GUILLOT
Poussette aussi!

BRÉTIGNY
Vous voilà libre alors? Guillot, je vous
en prie, n'allez pas m'enlever Manon!

GUILLOT
Vous enlever?

BRÉTIGNY
Non, jurez-moi que non!

GUILLOT
Laissons cette plaisanterie!
Mais dites moi, mon cher, on m'a
conté
A propos de Manon, que vous ayant
prié
De faire venir l'Opéra chez elle,
Vous avez, en dépit des larmes de la
belle,
Répondu: non.

BRÉTIGNY
C'est très vrai; la nouvelle est exacte!

GUILLOT
Il suffit; souffrez que je vous quitte
pour un instant, mais je reviendrai
vite.
(*Il sort en se frottant les mains et en
fredonnant.*)
Dig et dig et don,
On te la prendra ta Manon!
(*Brétigny, rentrée des Promeneurs et des
Marchands puis Manon, suivie de
sa chaise à porteurs, et accompagnée
d'un coureur, de deux petits nègres
et de porteurs à grande livrée.*)

ENSEMBLE
Voici les élégantes,
Les belles indolentes,
Maîtresses des coeurs,
Aux regards vainqueurs!

PROMENEURS
Quelle est cette princesse?
C'est au moins une duchesse!

FEMMES
Eh! ne savez-vous pas son nom?
C'est Manon, la belle Manon!

BRÉTIGNY ET SEIGNEURS
Ravissante Manon!

MANON
Suis-je gentille ainsi?

LES SEIGNEURS
Adorable, divine!

MANON
Est-ce vrai? Grand merci!
Je consens, vu, que je suis bonne,
A laisser admirer ma charmante per-
sonne!

Je marche sur tous les chemins
Aussi bien qu'une souveraine;
On s'incline, on baise mes mains,
Car par la beauté je suis reine!

Mes chevaux courent à grands pas;
Devant ma vie aventureuse,
Les grands s'avancent chapeau bas;
Je suis belle, je suis hereuse!

Autour de moi, tout doit fleurir!
Je vais à tout ce qui m'attire!
Et si Manon devait jamais mourir,
Ce serait, mes amis, dans un éclat
de rire!

LES SEIGNEURS
Bravo! Manon!

MANON
Obéissons quand leur voix appelle
Aux tendres amours, toujours, toujours!
Tant que vous êtes belle,
Usez sans les compter vos jours!

Profitons bien de la jeunesse,
Des jours qu'amène le printemps;
Aimons, rions, chantons sans cesse,
Nous n'avons encore que vingt ans!

BRÉTIGNY AND SEIGNEURS
Profitons bien de la jeunesse!
Aimons, rions, chantons sans cesse,
Nous n'avons encore que vingt ans! Ah!
Ah!

MANON
Le coeur, hélas! Le plus fidèle,
Oublie en un jour l'amour,
Et la jeunesse ouvrant son aile
A disparu sans retour.
(*à Brétigny*)
Et maintenant restez seul un instant;
Je veux faire ici quelqu' emplette.

BRÉTIGNY
Avec vous disparaît tout l'éclat de la
fête!

BRÉTIGNY

But when you go away, life's no longer
   amusing!

MANON

You're so gallant, and how often you
   show it;
Ev'ry noble Seigneur thinks he must
   be a poet!
(*Manon goes toward the shops at the
   rear. A few of the people follow, and
   then gradually drift away.*)
(*The Count Des Grieux appears from
   among the crowd.*)

BRÉTIGNY

If I am not mistaken, you are the
   Count Des Grieux?

THE COUNT

Monsieur de Brétigny?

BRÉTIGNY

I am. I can hardly believe my eyes!
You, in Paris!

THE COUNT

It's because of my son.

BRÉTIGNY

The Chevalier?

THE COUNT

He is not Chevalier any more. The
   Abbé Des Grieux is his title now . . .

MANON

(*approaches, while pretending to talk
         to a vendor*)
Des Grieux!

BRÉTIGNY

He is an Abbé! How did that happen?

THE COUNT

Heaven called him. He wants to enter
   holy orders.
He is at St. Sulpice. This evening he
   will give his discourse at the Sorbonne.

(*Manon withdraws.*)

BRÉTIGNY (*smiling*)

Abbé! That surprises me. What a
   change!

THE COUNT (*also smiling*)

You are the one who caused all this by
   managing to break up his love affair
   with a certain young lady.

BRÉTIGNY (*pointing to Manon*)

Speak softly.

THE COUNT

Is that the girl?

BRÉTIGNY

Yes, that is Manon.

THE COUNT (*lightly*)

Now I can see why you were so anxious
   to protect my son. (*seeing Manon
   approach*) But if you'll excuse me I
   think she wishes to speak with you.
   (*He bows, and steps away.*) (*aside*)
She is really quite beautiful.

MANON (*to Brétigny*)

My friend, I would like to have a
   bracelet to match this, but I can't
   find one.

BRÉTIGNY

All right, I'll go and see about it.
   (*He goes out, bowing to the Count.*)

THE COUNT (*aside*)

She is charming. I see why men fall in
   love with her.

MANON (*embarrassed, to the Count*)

Forgive me if I intrude
But I chanced to be near you.
Please do not think me rude;
I could not help but hear you.

THE COUNT (*smiling*)

There is nothing to forgive.
I quite understand. (*He bows, starting
   to withdraw.*)
Madame!

MANON

You were discussing a romance
That is over?

THE COUNT (*surprised*)

We were.

MANON

That's what I thought.
I hope that I do not offend you.
I know that the Abbé Des Grieux
Was in love for a while . . .

THE COUNT

With whom?

MANON

One of my friends.

THE COUNT

So! Go on!

MANON

Une fadeur! C'est du dernier galant!
On n'est pas grand seigneur sans être
    un peu poète!

(*Elle s'éloigne et se dirige vers les
    petites boutiques du fond du théâ-
    tre, escortée des curieux qui sortent
    peu à peu.*)

(*Brétigny, le Comte, Manon, au fond*)

BRÉTIGNY

Je ne me trompe pas, le comte Des
    Grieux?

LE COMTE

Monsieur de Brétigny?

BRÉTIGNY

Moi-même; c'est à peine si je puis en
    croire mes yeux! Vous à Paris?

LE COMTE

C'est mon fils qui m'amène.

BRÉTIGNY

Le chevalier?

LE COMTE

Il n'est plus chevalier, c'est l'abbé Des
    Grieux qu'à présent il faut dire . . .

MANON

(*qui s'est rapprochée tout en feignant
    de parler à un marchand*)

Des Grieux!

BRÉTIGNY

Abbé! lui! comment . . .

LE COMTE

Le ciel l'attire! Dans les ordres, il veut
    entrer. Il est à Saint-Sulpice, et, ce
    soir en Sorbonne, il prononce un dis-
    cours.

(*Manon s'éloigne.*)

BRÉTIGNY (*souriant*)

Abbé! cela m'étonne; un pareil change-
    ment!

LE COMTE (*souriant aussi*)

C'est vous qui l'avez fait,
En vous chargeant de briser net
L'amour qui l'attachait à certaine per-
    sonne . . .

BRÉTIGNY

(*montrant Manon qui est au fond*)

Plus bas!

LE COMTE

C'est elle?

BRÉTIGNY

Oui, c'est Manon.

LE COMTE (*raillant*)

Je devine alors la raison qui vous fit,
    avec tant de zèle, prendre les intérêts
    de mon fils . . .

(*voyant Manon qui se rapproche*)

Mais, pardon, elle veut vous parler . . .

(*Il salue et s'éloigne.*)

Elle est vraiment fort belle!

MANON (*à Brétigny*)

Je voudrais, mon ami,
Avoir un bracelet pareil à celui-ci.

Je ne puis le trouver.

BRÉTIGNY

C'est bien, je vais moi-même.

(*Il salue Le Comte et sort.*)

LE COMTE

Elle est charmante et je comprends
    qu'on l'aime!

MANON (*avec embarras*)

Pardon! mais j'étais là . . .près de vous,
    à deux pas . . .
J'entendais malgré moi . . . je suis très
    curieuse . . .

LE COMTE (*souriant*)

C'est un petit défaut, très petit ici-bas.

(*saluant*)

Madame!

MANON

Il s'agissait d'une histoire amoureuse?

LE COMTE

Mais oui.

MANON

C'est que je crois . . .
Pardonnez-moi, je vous en prie . . .
Que cet abbé . . . Des Grieux, autre-
    fois aimait . . .

LE COMTE

Qui donc?

MANON

Elle était mon amie.

LE COMTE

Ah! très bien!

MANON

He loved her and I would like to know
Has he been cured of his infatuation?
Oh tell me, if you will,
Is he free at last?
Has he torn from his heart
All the memories of the past?

THE COUNT

You are asking more than I can tell
you.
What becomes of youth and love
And the summer when it closes,
And whither goes the sweet perfume
of roses?

MANON (aside)

Dear God, give me strength, give me
courage
To ask him all that I must know!

THE COUNT

When the past can be forgotten,
It is sometimes wiser not to know.

MANON

And may I ask you: do you believe
that he has suffered?
Does he never mention her name?

THE COUNT (looking at her steadily)

If he weeps, he weeps in silence.

MANON (deeply moved)

Does he say she was to blame?

THE COUNT

No!

MANON

And has he told you that she loved him
With all her heart?

THE COUNT

The pain and suffering have cured him
And made him strong.

MANON

But how—

THE COUNT

Your friend has set him an example,
And I'm sure you will agree
It is a wise one.
He has learned to forget.
(The Count bows, and withdraws.)

MANON (to herself)

To forget!
(Enter lords and ladies of fashion,
promenaders, vendors, Brétigny and
Guillot with friends; then later, Lescaut.)

BRÉTIGNY

Answer me, Guillot! (Laughter)

GUILLOT

Never! But he laughs best who laughs
last.

BRÉTIGNY

Monsieur de Morfontaine, you must
tell me everything.

GUILLOT

To you, my friend, nothing.
(to Manon) But to you, oh my
queen . . .

BRÉTIGNY

What?

GUILLOT

All right, I will!
The Opera which you would not bring
to her—in just a moment will be
here!
(commotion in the crowd)

BRÉTIGNY

I give up! (to Manon) You are sad!

MANON

Oh, no!

BRÉTIGNY

I believe I see some tears.

MANON

Nonsense!

GUILLOT

Come here, Manon, over here if you
please.
Now they will dance for you our very
new ballet.
Lescaut, come here!

LESCAUT

Here I am, at your service.

GUILLOT

My friend, this party is on me.
I'll buy a round of drinks for all the
people.
(takes out his purse) How much?

LESCAUT

(as he takes the purse and goes out)

We'll count up later on.

BRÉTIGNY, NOBLEMEN, CROWD OF MEN
AND WOMEN

The ballet! The ballet is here!
Every one give them a cheer!
The Opera ballet is here!

MANON

Il l'aimait, et je voudrais savoir
Si sa raison sortit victorieuse . . .
Et si de l'oublieuse
Il a pu parvenir
A chasser de son coeur le cruel souvenir?

LE COMTE

Faut-il donc savoir tant de choses?
Que deviennent les plus beaux jours,
Où vont les premières amours,
Où vole le parfum des roses?

MANON (à part)

Mon Dieu, donnez-moi le courage
De tout oser lui demander!

LE COMTE

Ignorer n'est-il pas plus sage,
Au passé pourquoi s'attarder?

MANON

Un mot encore! . . . A-t-il souffert de
son absence?
Vous a-t-il dit parfois son nom?

LE COMTE
(la regardant fixement)

Ses larmes coulaint en silence.

MANON (très émue)

L'a-t-il maudite, en pleurant?

LE COMTE

Non!

MANON

Vous a-t-il dit que la parjure
L'avait aimé?

LE COMTE

Son coeur, guéri de sa blessure,
S'est refermé!

MANON

Mais depuis?

LE COMTE

Il a fait ainsi que votre amie,
Ce que l'on doit faire ici-bas,
Quand on est sage, n'est-ce pas?
On oublie!
(Le Comte salue respectueusement et
se retire.)

MANON (douloureusement)

On oublie!
(Brétigny et Guillot sont accompagnés
de quelques amis.)

BRÉTIGNY

Répondez-moi, Guillot! (On rit.)

GUILLOT

Jamais! Mais rira bien qui rira le
dernier!

BRÉTIGNY

Monsieur de Morfontaine, vous allez
tout me dire!

GUILLOT

A vous, mon ami, rien!
(se tournant vers Manon)
Mais à vous, ô ma reine!

BRÉTIGNY

Plaît-il?

GUILLOT

Eh bien! oui . . . l'Opéra que vous lui
refusiez . . . il sera dans un instant
ici.

BRÉTIGNY

Je dois rendre les armes! . . .
(à Manon)
Vous êtes triste!

MANON

Oh! non!

BRÉTIGNY

On dirait que des larmes . . .

MANON

Folie!

GUILLOT

Allons, Manon, approchez, s'il vous
plaît,
On va danser pour vous notre nouveau ballet!
Lescaut, venez!

LESCAUT

Je suis là pour vous plaire.

GUILLOT

Veillez . . . le tout est à mes frais,
A ce qu'on donne à boire au populaire.
(tirant sa bourse)
Combien?

LESCAUT
(la prenant et saluant)

Nous compterons après!

SEIGNEURS ET BOURGEOIS

Voici l' Opéra!
Tous Paris en parlera!
C'est le ballet de l'Opéra!
C'est un plaisir de souveraine.

BRÉTIGNY

Oh what delight, oh what a pleasure!
My friend Guillot will be in debt!
He has bought up the Opera!

GUILLOT (*aside, gleefully*)

Oh what delight, oh what a pleasure!
I have brought the whole Opera
Just for Manon, my little treasure!
This, my friend, you won't forget!

MANON (*to herself, disturbed*)

No! His life and my own are forever
  bound together!
He cannot have forgotten me . . .
(*to Lescaut*) Cousin! My carriage!

LESCAUT

Where are you going?

MANON

To St. Sulpice.

LESCAUT

What is this bizarre caprice? Pardon
me if I make you repeat it. To St.
Sulpice?

MANON

To St. Sulpice.

GUILLOT

How do you like all this, mistress of my
  heart?

MANON

I have seen nothing!

GUILLOT

Nothing! That's the price of gallantry.
Is that all I deserve?

SCENE II

*The reception room of the seminary of
St. Sulpice. A reverent group of women, both aristocrats and common-
ers, are seen leaving the seminary
chapel.*

THE WOMEN

How very moving!
How wonderful to hear!
And so improving!
How simple and how clear!
His gentle voice, sweet and sincere!
Sweet and sincere, filled with emotion!
And with every word, my dear,
My inmost heart was stirred
To a deeper devotion!
How well he described, in stating his
  thesis,

St. Augustine's life, and saintly
  Theresa's!
He truly is a saint!
A saint he must be!
My dear, you will surely agree!

THE WOMEN (*reverently*)

It is he! The Abbé Des Grieux comes
  by
With thoughtful mein and downcast
  eye!
(*The women leave, after acknowledg-
ing Des Grieux's presence with deep
respect.*)

THE COUNT

Bravo, my son, a great success! Our
family should be proud to number
among its members a new Bossuet!

DES GRIEUX

Please, father, spare me that! (*silence*)

THE COUNT

Is it for the best, my son, that you
contemplate binding yourself to
heaven forever?

DES GRIEUX

Yes, I have found in life only bitterness and disgust.

THE COUNT

Those are strong-sounding words!
But my son, how have you been living?
What do you really know of life
That you wish to finish like this?
I beg of you to take a wife
Worthy of us, worthy of you.
Take up the joys of family life
As I did, as you ought to do.
For heaven does not ask for any more
That is your duty!
To give up the world and hide away
Is sometimes not a virtue at all.

DES GRIEUX

Nothing can prevent me from taking
my vows.

THE COUNT

It's done, then?

DES GRIEUX

Yes, that's the way I want it.

THE COUNT

So! Then I will go through this iron
gate and tell the brethren that they
have a new saint in the family. I'm
quite sure they won't believe it.

BRÉTIGNY

C'est un plaisir de souveraine,
L'ami Guillot se ruinera!

GUILLOT

C'est un plaisir de souveraine,
Avoir fait venir l'Opéra
Et son ballet au Cours la Reine,
Mon rival enragera!

MANON

(à part, après le ballet)

Non, sa vie à la mienne est pour jamais liée!
Il ne peut m'avoir oubliée . . .

(voyant Lescaut près d'elle)

Ma chaise, mon cousin.

LESCAUT

Où faut-il vous porter, cousine?

MANON

A Saint-Sulpice!

LESCAUT

Quel est ce bizarre caprice?
Pardonnez-moi de faire répéter . . .
A Saint-Sulpice?

MANON

A Saint-Sulpice!

GUILLOT

Eh bien, maîtresse de ma vie,
Qu'en dites-vous?

MANON

Je n'ai rien vu!

GUILLOT

(mécontent s'éloignant)

Rien vu? . . . voilà le prix de ma galanterie! . . .
Est-ce là ce qui m'était dû?

DEUXIÈME TABLEAU

Le parloir du séminaire à Saint-Sulpice.

GRANDES DAMES, BOURGEOISES, DÉVOTES

Quelle éloquence,
L'admirable orateur!
Quelle abondance,
Le grand prédicateur!
Ah! dans sa voix quelle douceur,
Quelle douceur et quelle flamme!
Comme en l'écoutant, la ferveur
Pénètre doucement jusqu'au fond de nos âmes!
De quel art divin
Il a, dans sa thèse,

Peint Saint Augustin
Et Sainte Thérèse!
Lui-même est un saint,
C'est un fait certain,
N'est-ce pas, ma chère!

(Entre Des Grieux.)

LES DAMES

C'est lui, c'est l'abbé Des Grieux,
Voyez comme il baisse les yeux!

(Les dames sortent peu à peu et saluent Des Grieux avec de profondes révérences.)

LE COMTE

Bravo, mon cher, succès complet,
Notre maison doit être fière
D'avoir parmi les siens un nouveau Bossuet!

DES GRIEUX

De grâce, épargnez-moi, mon père!

(Un silence)

LE COMTE

Et, c'est pour de bon, chevalier,
Que tu prétends au ciel pour jamais te lier?

DES GRIEUX

Oui, je n'ai trouvé dans la vie
Qu'amertume et dégoût.

LE COMTE

Les grands mots que voilà!
Quelle route as-tu donc suivie?
Et que sais-tu de cette vie
Pour penser qu'elle finit là?
Epouse quelque brave fille,
Digne de nous, digne de toi;
Deviens un père de famille
Ni pire, ni meilleur que moi;
Le ciel n'en veut pas davantage;
C'est là le devoir, entends-tu?
La vertu qui fait du tapage
N'est déjà plus de la vertu!

DES GRIEUX

Rien ne peut m'empêcher de prononcer mes voeux!

LE COMTE

C'est dit alors?

DES GRIEUX

Oui, je le veux!

LE COMTE

Soit! Je franchirai donc seul cette grille,
Et vais leur annoncer là-bas.
Qu'ils ont un saint dans la famille . . .
J'en sais beaucoup qui ne me croiront pas!

DES GRIEUX

Please do not make fun of me!

THE COUNT (*moved*)

One word more! Since it is not certain
that they will give you a benefice or
an abbey right away, I will send you
thirty thousand francs tonight.

DES GRIEUX

Father!

THE COUNT

It's yours. It comes to you from your
mother's estate. And now, farewell
my son.

DES GRIEUX

Goodbye, father.

THE COUNT

Goodbye. . . . Stay here and pray. (*He
goes out.*)

DES GRIEUX

I am alone, alone at last,
This is my hour of destiny!
The one thing I desire
Is the blessed peace of God
That can still make me whole.
Yes, I have set the Lord of Heaven
Between the world and my soul.

Leave me now, lovely dream,
Still too lovely and dear,
Let my soul be at peace.
Peace, oh, so dearly won!
I have drunk from a cup
Poisoned by sin and fear;
I have sought some release,
Seeking, and finding none!
Leave me, leave me now,
Lovely dream!
What care I for this life
And dreams of love and glory!
Let the vows I have made
Be the end of the story,
Let me forget that name
That pursues me even now!

THE PORTER OF THE SEMINARY

The service is starting.

DES GRIEUX

I will come.
Dear Lord, through thy great merit,
O purify my spirit!
Let that dark shadow now depart,
That which is hiding still
In the depths of my heart!
(*He goes out slowly.*)

THE PORTER

He is young. . . . He seems to be sincere.
He has made a deep impression on
the most beautiful ladies of the con-
gregation!
(*Enter Manon.*)

MANON (*tensely*)

Monsieur, I wish to speak to the Abbé
Des Grieux.

PORTER

Very well.

MANON (*giving him money*)

Take this.
(*The Porter goes out.*)
These silent walls! This cold air!
If only all this has not already changed
him! If only he has not yet learned
to hate me, and to curse my name!

CHOIR (*in the chapel*)

Magnificat anima mea Dominum,
Et exultavit spiritus meus.

MANON (*listening*)

They are praying. Ah, I would like to
pray!

Pardon, O Lord, blessed Father in
heaven
If I dare offer a prayer
That all my sins may be forgiven.
If a voice from so low can be heard up
above
I implore Thee to give back the heart
of my love.

CHOIR (*in the chapel*)

In Deo salutari meo.
(*Des Grieux enters and comes forward.*)

MANON

It's he!
(*She turns away. She is nearly overcome with emotion.*)

DES GRIEUX

You! No!

MANON

Yes, it is I!

DES GRIEUX

What are you doing here?
Go away! Let me alone!

MANON (*sorrowfully*)

Yes, you have the right to refuse me,
Yet you loved me well in the past.
Ah! cannot the lips that accuse me
Speak pardon for my sin at last?

DES GRIEUX

Ne raillez pas, monsieur, je vous en
prie!

LE COMTE (*ému*)

Un mot encor! Comme il n'est pas
certain que l'on te donne ici, du jour
au lendemain, un bénéfice, une ab-
baye, je vais dès ce soir t'envoyer
trente mille livres . . .

DES GRIEUX

Mon père . . .

LE COMTE

C'est à toi, c'est ta part sur la bien de
ta mère; et maintenant . . . adieu,
mon fils!

DES GRIEUX

Adieu, mon père!

LE COMTE

Adieu . . . reste à prier!

(*Il sort.*)

DES GRIEUX

Je suis seul! enfin! C'est le
moment suprême!
Il n'est plus rien que j'aime
Que le repos sacré que m'apporte la
foi!
Oui, j'ai voulu mettre Dieu même
Entre le monde et moi!

Ah! fuyez, douce image à mon âme
trop chère;
Respectez un repos cruellement gagné,
Et songez si j'ai bu dans une coupe
amère,
Que mon coeur l'emplirait
de ce qu'il a saigné!

Que m'importe la vie et ce semblant
de gloire?
Je ne veux que chasser du fond de ma
mémoire
Un nom maudit . . . Ce nom qui m'ob-
sède . . . et pourquoi?

LE PORTIER

C'est l'office!

DES GRIEUX

J'y vais!

Mon Dieu, de votre flamme
Purifiez mon âme . . .
Et dissipez à sa lueur
L'ombre qui passe encore dans le fond
de mon coeur!

(*Il sort.*)

LE PORTIER

Il est jeune . . . et sa foi semble sincère
. . . il a fait grand émoi parmi les
plus belles de nos fidèles!

(*Entre Manon.*)

MANON (*à demi voilée, avec effort*)

Monsieur . . . je veux parler . . . à
l'abbé Des Grieux!

LE PORTIER

Fort bien.

MANON

Tenez!

(*Le portier sort.*)

Ces murs silencieux . . .
Cet air froid qu'on respire . . .
Pourvu que tout cela n'ait pas changé
son coeur!
Devenu sans pitié pour une folle er-
reur,
Pourvu qu'il n'ait pas appris à mau-
dire!

CHOEUR (*de la chapelle*)

Magnificat anima mea Dominum
Et exultavit spiritus meus.

MANON

Là-bas . . . on prie . . . Ah! je voudrais
prier!
Pardonnez-moi, Dieu de toute puis-
sance,
Car si j'ose vous supplier
En implorant votre clémence,
Si ma voix de si bas peut monter
jusqu'aux cieux,
C'est pour vous demander le coeur de
Des Grieux!

CHOEUR

In Dea salutari meo.

(*Des Grieux entre par le fond.*)

MANON

C'est lui!

(*Elle se retourne et ferme son voile.
Elle est prête à défaillir.*)

DES GRIEUX

Toi! vous!

MANON

Oui, c'est moi!

DES GRIEUX

Que viens-tu faire ici!
Va-t'en, éloigne-toi!

MANON (*suppliante*)

Oui, je fus cruelle et coupable
Mais rappelez-vous tant d'amour!
Ah! dans ce regard qui m'accable,
Lirai-je mon pardon un jour?

DES GRIEUX

No! That love could only enslave us,
That dream doomed to vanish away,
Love that heaven never truly gave us
But for just a moment, just a day!
Oh, unfaithful Manon!

MANON (*approaching*)

Perhaps I could repent . . .

DES GRIEUX

Oh, unfaithful, unfaithful!

MANON

Could you not find some pity in your
heart?

DES GRIEUX (*interrupting her*)

You think that I believe you!
No! At last I have banished you from
my memory
As well as from my heart.

MANON

Alas! The bird in flight
That gaily has arisen
So often returns at night
To beat at the doors of its prison.
Forgive me now!

DES GRIEUX

No!

MANON

I'll die if you refuse.
I shall live once again
If you say that you love me.

DES GRIEUX

No, you have killed my love!

MANON

Is your soul in the sky,
Your heart so high above me?
Listen to me! Can you forget?

Is this not my hand?
Can't you feel it pressing?
Is it not my voice?
Are these not my arms
Tenderly caressing?
Have you made your choice
And these eyes of mine
That could always charm you,
Can their helpless tears
Nevermore disarm you?
Am I not the same?
Don't you know my name?
Ah, look in my eyes.
Am I not Manon?

DES GRIEUX

O Lord, support me now!
Ah, do not let me falter!

MANON

I love you!

DES GRIEUX

Ah, be still!
You must not speak of love in here
So near the altar!

MANON

I love you!
(*A bell sounds.*)

DES GRIEUX

It is the hour of prayer
And I ought to be there!

MANON

No! I will not leave you now.
Is it not my hand?
Can't you feel it pressing.
Just as in the past?

DES GRIEUX

Just as in the past.

MANON

And these eyes of mine
That could always charm you,
Are they not the same?

DES GRIEUX

All as in the past.

MANON

Now look in my eyes!
Do you know my name?
Am I not Manon?

DES GRIEUX (*with spirit*)

Ah, Manon! How can I resist
All that my heart desires?

MANON

At last!

DES GRIEUX

Though my soul may be lost,
Ah, let the heavens fall!
My life is in your heart,
My life is in your eyes!
Come, Manon! I love you!

MANON

I love you!

ACT FOUR

*The Hotel Transylvania in Paris. The
gambling rooms.*

THE DEALERS (*at the card table*)

Make your play, gentlemen!

DES GRIEUX

Non! j'avais écrit sur le sable
Ce rêve insensé d'un amour
Que le ciel n'avait fait durable
Que pour un instant, pour un jour!
Ah! perfide Manon!

MANON (*se rapprochant*)

Si je me repentais . . .

DES GRIEUX

Ah! perfide! perfide!

MANON

Est-ce que tu n'aurais pas de pitié?

DES GRIEUX (*l'interrompant*)

Je ne veux pas vous croire.
Non, vous êtes sortie enfin de ma mé-
moire
Ainsi que de mon coeur!

MANON

Hélas! l'oiseau qui fuit
Ce qu'il croit l'esclavage,
Le plus souvent la nuit
D'un vol désespéré revient battre au
vitrage!
Pardonne-moi.

DES GRIEUX

Non!

MANON

Je meurs à tes genoux!
Rends-moi ton amour si tu veux que
je vive!

DES GRIEUX

Non! il est mort pour vous!

MANON

L'est-il donc à ce point que rien ne le
ravive!
Ecoute-moi! Rappelle-toi!

N'est ce plus ma main que cette main
presse?
N'est-ce plus ma voix?
N'est-elle pour toi plus une caresse,
Tout comme autrefois,
Et ces yeux, jadis pour toi pleins de
charmes?
Ne brillent-ils plus à travers mes lar-
mes?
Ne suis-je plus moi? N'ai-je plus mon
nom?
Ah! regarde-moi! N'est-ce plus Ma-
non?

DES GRIEUX

O Dieu! Soutenez-moi dans cet instant
suprême!

MANON

Je t'aime!

DES GRIEUX

Tais-toi!
Ne parle pas d'amour ici, c'est un
blasphème!

MANON

Je t'aime!

DES GRIEUX

C'est l'heure de prier . . . on m'appelle
là-bas . . .

MANON

Non, je ne te quitterai pas!
(*Des Grieux revient ramené vers Ma-
non, comme par une force invin-
cible.*)
Viens! N'est-ce plus ma main
Que cette main presse,
Tout comme autrefois?

DES GRIEUX

Tout comme autrefois!

MANON

Et ses yeux, jadis
Pour toi pleins de charmes,
N'est-ce plus Manon?

DES GRIEUX

Tout comme autrefois!

MANON

Ah! Regarde moi!
Ne suis-je plus moi?
N'est-ce plus Manon?

DES GRIEUX (*avec élan*)

Ah, Manon! Je ne veux plus lutter
contre moi-même!

MANON

Enfin!

DES GRIEUX

Et dussé-je sur moi faire crouler les
cieux,
Ma vie est dans ton coeur, ma vie est
dans tes yeux!
Ah! viens, Manon, je t'aime!

MANON

Je t'aime!

ACTE QUATRIÈME
L'Hôtel de Transylvanie

*Une grande et luxueuse salle de l'hô-
tel. Des tables de jeu sont établies
dans· cette salle et dans les autres
salons.*

LES CROUPIERS (*répètent au fond*)

Faites vos jeux, messieurs!

FIRST GAMBLER
A thousand pistoles!

SECOND GAMBLER
Taken!

FIRST GAMBLER
I double it!

SECOND GAMBLER
Play!

FIRST GAMBLER
Lost! Two!

SECOND GAMBLER
Five!

FIRST GAMBLER
Seven!

SECOND GAMBLER
Ten!

A VOICE (upstage)
A hundred louis!

LESCAUT
Four hundred louis!
Hurrah! I win!

A GAMBLER (pursuing Lescaut)
I tell you, that's my money!

LESCAUT
When someone says that to me, and
seems so sure of it . . .

GAMBLER
I have the ace and the king!

LESCAUT
All right! Let's begin again.
It's all the same to me!
(The Sharpers come cautiously for-
ward.)

THE SHARPERS
It's a foolhardy gambler
Who lets chance play a part;
But we who know our business
Think that gambling's an art;
Fortune holds no terrors,
Be she cruel or kind!
There are ways we can find
To rectify her errors!

LESCAUT
(putting the money in his pocket)
I've always played an honest game
And I shall always do the same!

POUSSETTE, JAVOTTE, ROSETTE
(observing the games as they stroll
about.)
Here we are at the Transylvania!

Come, one and all! Everyone's invited!
Everyone's sure to be delighted!
Day after day, night after night,
Gold is the prize for the fairest,
And we're the lucky ones tonight!
(Lescaut returns in triumph. The
Sharpers and the women surround
him eagerly.)

LESCAUT
There's a lady, dearest and rarest,
And it's here that she chooses to dwell.
Many a sonnet and villanelle
I have composed, all for my fairest,
Honoring her I love so well!
(clink of gold coins)
And that's the chime, the golden chime
That fittingly blends with my rhyme!
Let me describe her—
Though I seldom discuss any lady I've
met,
I think I could reveal her name.
And yet. . . .

THE WOMEN
Tell us her name!

LESCAUT
Queen of Spades, the card of good
fortune!
And that's the end of my chansonette.

(clink of coins, as before)

THE WOMEN, LESCAUT, THE SHARPERS
And that's the chime, the golden
chime
That fittingly ends the rhyme!
(Guillot enters.)

GUILLOT (to Lescaut)
Bravo, my lad!

LESCAUT
Thanks!
(The Sharpers go back to the faro
table, the Gamblers begin the game
again.)

GUILLOT
(to Lescaut and the women)
I too have written verses from time to
time,
And once I did a naughty rhyme
On the Regent's affair
With a word here and there
Omitted, the dangerous parts left out!
Now you shall see just what it's all
about . . .

UN JOUEUR

Mille pistoles!

DEUXIÈME JOUEUR

C'est tenu!

PREMIER JOUEUR

Je double!

DEUXIÈME

Brelan!

PREMIER

C'est perdu! Deux! . . .

DEUXIÈME

Cinq!

PREMIER

Sept!

DEUXIÈME

Dix!

UNE VOIX

Cent louis!

LESCAUT

Quatre cent louis!
Vivat! . . . j'ai gagné.

UN JOUEUR

Je vous jure que l'argent m'appartient!

LESCAUT

Du moment qu'on l'assure avec autant
    d'aplomb . . .

LE JOUEUR

J'avais l'as et le roi!

LESCAUT

Recommençons alors, ça m'est égal à
    moi!

LES AIGREFINS

Le joueur sans prudence
Livre tout au hasard;
Mais le vrai sage pense
Que jouer est un art!
Pour la rendre opportune,
Nous savons sans danger,
Quand il faut corriger
L'erreur de la fortune!

LESCAUT

Tout en jouant honnêtement,
Je n'ai jamais fait autrement!

POUSSETTE, JAVOTTE ET ROSETTE

A l'Hôtel de Transylvanie,

Accourez tous, on vous en prie;
A l'Hôtel de Transylvanie
Passez vos jours, passez vos nuits.
L'or vient tout seul aux plus belles,
C'est nous qui gagnons toujours!

LESCAUT

C'est ici que celle que j'aime
A daigné fixer son séjour,
Et je vous dirai quelque jour
Certains couplets que j'ai, moi-même,
Faits en l'honneur de notre amour.

(Bruit de l'or)

Et c'est ce bruit, ce bruit charmant
Qui leur sert d'accompagnement.
Celle que j'aime, . . . je me pique
D'être plein de discrétion . . .
Pourtant, je vous dirai son nom:

LES FEMMES

Oui, son nom!

LESCAUT

C'est Pallas, la dame de pique!
Et là s'arrête ma chanson . . .

(Bruit de l'or)

TOUS

Et c'est ce bruit, ce bruit charmant,
Qui lui sert d'accompagnement!

(Guillot vient d'entrer.)

GUILLOT (à Lescaut)

Bravo, mon cher!

LESCAUT

Merci.

GUILLOT

J'enfourche aussi Pégase
De temps en temps. Ainsi, moi, j'ai
    sur le régent
Fait des vers très malins, mais, en
    homme prudent je gaze
Et passe les mots dangereux,
Vous allez voir, on ne comprend que
    mieux!

GUILLOT

"When the . . ."

(*He hums, making gestures to portray the character.*)

That's the Regent!

(*resuming the song*)

"Goes to see . . ."

(*same business with pantomime and humming*)

That's his mistress!

"Then says he . . ." (*same business*)

Do you all see? . . .

"Then says she. . . . Your noble Highness! . . ."

Tra-la-la la!

(*to those listening*)

Ah! It is bright, it is gay!

LESCAUT AND THE THREE WOMEN
(*laughing*)

And you do not get caught that way!

GUILLOT

Ah! It is bright, it is sharp, it is gay!

ALL

Sh! . . . .

(*There is much noise as more people come in. Everyone looks to see who is coming.*)

(*Manon and Des Grieux enter the hall.*)

GUILLOT

Who has arrived to cause so much excitement?

POUSSETTE, JAVOTTE AND ROSETTE

It is lovely Manon with her dear chevalier.

DES GRIEUX (*looking around*)

Why am I here! When I tried to refuse,
I had not the strength to resist her.

GUILLOT (*annoyed*)

Des Grieux!

LESCAUT (*to Guillot*)

Your face is changing color!
Something here seems to be bothering you.

GUILLOT

I have a right to be angry.
I adored Manon and it hurts and infuriates me
That she loves someone else who is taking my place!

THE DEALERS

Make your play, gentlemen!

(*All return to the game. Manon and Des Grieux stand together away from the crowd. Manon, seeing that Des Grieux is not happy, comes to him.*)

MANON

Tell me now, Des Grieux, am I still your beloved?

DES GRIEUX

Manon, siren and sphinx calling man to destruction,
Many women in one, how I love you and hate you!
Gold is your heart's desire, and pleasure is your god!
But yet, in spite of all, oh, how I love you!

MANON

And I . . . Oh, how I would adore you, if you'll agree . . .

DES GRIEUX

If I agree? . . .

MANON

Our store of money now is gone,
Chevalier, gambled all away!
But, my friend, if only you would play,
Another fortune quickly might be won.

DES GRIEUX

What are you saying, Manon?

LESCAUT

Manon is right.
The faro table is the one!
Another fortune quickly might be won.

DES GRIEUX

You want me to play? Not I! Not I!

LESCAUT

You are quite wrong! Manon would not like to be poor.

MANON

Chevalier, if you really love me,
Give in, and soon you'll see
That we are sure to win.

LESCAUT

You're sure to win!
Lady Luck is often quite contrary.
From a gambler who plays every day
She will take all her favors away,
And she often picks her winners
From the rankest beginners.

GUILLOT

"Quand le . . .

(*Il tousse.*)

C'est le Régent.

"Va voir . . .

(*Il tousse.*)

C'est sa maîtresse.

"Il dit . . .

(*Il tousse.*)

On me comprend . . .

"Elle répond . . .

(*Il tousse.*)

De Votre Altesse!

Tra-la-la-la!

C'est badin, c'est léger!

LESCAUT ET LES FEMMES (*en riant*)

Et l'on ne court aucun danger!

GUILLOT

Ah! C'est piquant! C'est badin! C'est
léger!

TOUS

Chut! . . .

(*Grand tapage, tout le monde se lève
pour regarder les personnes qui entrent.*)

(*Les Mêmes, Manon, Des Grieux*)

GUILLOT

Mais qui donc nous arrive et fait tout
ce tapage?

POUSSETTE, JAVOTTE ET ROSETTE

C'est la belle Manon avec son chevalier.

DES GRIEUX

(*regardant autour de lui*)

M'y voici donc! J'aurais dû résister!
Je n'en ai pas eu le courage.

GUILLOT (*vexé*)

Le chevalier!

LESCAUT (*à Guillot*)

Vous changez de visage,
Et quelque chose, ici, parait vous ir-
riter . . .

GUILLOT

A bon droit je fais la grimace,
Car j'adorais Manon, et je trouve
blessant et froissant
Qu'elle en aime un autre à ma place!

LES CROUPIERS

Faites vos jeux, messieurs!

(*Tout le monde retourne au jeu. Manon et Des Grieux sont restés iso-
lés sur le devant de la scène. Manon voyant que Des Grieux con-
tinue d'être triste, s'approche de lui.*)

MANON

De ton coeur, Des Grieux, suis-je plus
souveraine?

DES GRIEUX

Manon, sphinx étonnant, véritable
sirène!
Coeur trois fois féminin . . . que je
t'aime et te hais!
Pour le plaisir et l'or quelle ardeur
inouïe!
Ah! folle que tu es!
Comme je t'aime!

MANON

Et moi . . . comme je t'aimerais . . .
Si tu voulais . . .

DES GRIEUX

Si je voulais . . .

MANON

Notre opulence est envolée,
Chevalier, nous n'avons plus rien!
Mais ici, quand on le veut bien,
Une fortune est vite retrouvée.

DES GRIEUX

Que me dis-tu, Manon?

LESCAUT

Elle a raison!
En quelques coups de pharaon,
Une fortune est vite retrouvée.

DES GRIEUX

Qui? Moi? Jouer? Jamais, jamais!

LESCAUT

Vous avez tort, Manon n'aime pas la
misère.

MANON

Chevalier, si je te suis chère,
Consens, et tu verras qu'après
Nous serons riches!

LESCAUT

C'est probable!

La fortune n'est intraitable
Qu'avec le joueur éprouvé
Qui contre elle souvent a lutté!
Elle est douce, au contraire, à celui
qui commence!

MANON (*to Des Grieux*)
Won't you do it for me?

DES GRIEUX
O Manon, this is madness!

LESCAUT
Come on!

DES GRIEUX (*to Manon*)
I'm giving you my soul!

LESCAUT
You're sure to win.

DES GRIEUX (*to Manon*)
And will you give me more?

LESCAUT
You're sure to win!

MANON
I swear upon my life to love you more
than before!

DES GRIEUX
Manon, siren and sphinx calling man to
destruction,
Many women in one, how I love you
and hate you!
Gold is your heart's desire, and pleas-
ure is your god!
But yet, in spite of all, oh, how I love
you!
Must I for you give up my honor
And all that's dearest to my heart!
Even my very soul!

MANON
Oh, I will love you more than ever,
I'll give you all I have to give.
Ah, this is the way to live!
I swear on my life to love you forever.

LESCAUT
Fortune loves a beginner,
Come on and play, you'll be a winner.
To play and play again, that's how to
live!
With all you have to give!

GUILLOT
(*approaching with Javotte and
Poussette*)
(*to Des Grieux*)
Monsieur, shall we join in a game?
I would be honored to count you in.
Try me once more
And see if you're as lucky as before!

POUSSETTE
Bravo, Guillot, I bet that you will win!
JAVOTTE
And as for me, I'm betting on the
Chevalier.

GUILLOT (*to Des Grieux*)
Do you accept?

DES GRIEUX
I accept.
GUILLOT
Let's begin!
ROSETTE
Is the bet still on?

JAVOTTE AND ROSETTE
The bet is on.
GUILLOT
A thousand pistoles!

DES GRIEUX
Good, Monsieur! A thousand pistoles!

LESCAUT
A thousand pistoles!
Oh Lady Luck, be mine!
(*He goes to another table.*)

MANON
I am drunk with pleasure!
This is living!

POUSSETTE, JAVOTTE AND ROSETTE
This is living!
MANON
Or, at least, this is the life for me!
The sound of gold, of laughter,
Joy flowing all around!
(*Javotte hands her a glass of wine.*)
Let's live for today, like the rose!
Sing now, love now, for who knows . . .
Who knows what tomorrow may bring!
Sing now while there's time to sing!
Youth will quickly fly,
Beauty soon will die,
Let us take our pleasure
Before we're old!
Who would want to miss
Ev'n a single kiss!
As for me,
Let me see
Some gold!

GAMBLERS AND SHARPERS (*to Lescaut*)
Play!
LESCAUT
I haven't any cash, but I assure you
My credit here is good.

MANON (*à Des Grieux*)
Tu veux bien, n'est-ce pas?

DES GRIEUX
Infernale démence!

LESCAUT
Venez!

DES GRIEUX
Je t'aurai tout donné!

LESCAUT
Vous gagnerez!

DES GRIEUX
Mais qu'aurai-je en retour?

LESCAUT
Vous gagnerez!

MANON
Mon être tout entier, ma vie et mon
amour!

DES GRIEUX
Manon, sphinx étonnant, véritable
sirène!
Coeur trois fois feminin! Que je t'aime
et te hais!
Pour le plaisir et l'or quelle ardeur
inouïe!
Ah! folle que tu es, comme je t'aime!
Ah! faut-il donc que ma faiblesse
Te donne jusqu'à mon honneur!

MANON
Repose-toi sur ma tendresse!
Ne doute jamais de mon coeur!
Ah! c'est le notre bonheur!
Ne doute jamais! A toi mon amour!
A toi tout mon être!

LESCAUT
Votre chance est certain!
Jouez toujours! Jouez sans cesse!
Jouez toujours! C'est le bonheur!
Jouez encore! Venez! vous gagnerez!
(*Guillot rentre en scène avec Javotte
et Poussette.*)

GUILLOT (*à Des Grieux*)
Un mot, s'il vous plaît, chevalier!
Je vous propose une partie.
Nous verrons si sur moi vous devez
l'emporter toujours.

POUSSETTE
Bravo, Guillot, pour vous, moi, je parie!

JAVOTTE
Et je parie alors, moi, pour ce chevalier.

GUILLOT (*à Des Grieux*)
Acceptez-vous?

DES GRIEUX
J'accepte!

GUILLOT
Commençons!

POUSSETTE
Nous parions toujours!

JAVOTTE ET ROSETTE
Nous parions!

GUILLOT
Mille pistoles!

DES GRIEUX
Soit, monsieur, mille pistoles!

LESCAUT
Mille pistoles!
A moi, Pallas, à moi!
(*Il va se mettre à une autre table de
jeu.*)

MANON
Ces ivresses folles
C'est la vie, ou du moins c'est celle
que je veux!

POUSSETTE, JAVOTTE ET ROSETTE
C'est la vie!

MANON
Ce bruit de l'or, ce rire et ces éclats
joyeux!
A nous les amours et les roses!
(*prenant le verre que lui donne Ja-
votte*)
Chanter, aimer, sont douces choses,
Qui sait si nous vivrons demain!
La jeunesse passe,
La beauté s'efface.
Que tous nos désirs
Soient pour les plaisirs!
L'amour et ses fièvres,
Sur toutes les lèvres
Pour Manon encor
De l'or et de l'or!

LES JOUEURS (*à Lescaut*)
Au jeu!

LESCAUT
Permettez-moi de jouer sur parole,
Je suis de bonne foi!

GAMBLERS AND SHARPERS
Play!

LESCAUT
Not one pistole! In fact, nothing at all!
I have been robbed! Me!

GUILLOT (*to Des Grieux*)
Your kind of luck is most unusual!
One thousand louis more!

DES GRIEUX (*feverishly*)
Good, Monsieur! One thousand more!

GUILLOT
I lose!

MANON (*approaching the players*)
My dear, did you win?

DES GRIEUX
(*showing her gold and bills*)
Look here!

MANON
Is it ours?

DES GRIEUX
It is ours!

MANON
I adore you!

GUILLOT
Let's double, if you will?

DES GRIEUX
I will!

GUILLOT
I've lost again.

MANON (*to Des Grieux*)
My dear, did I not say
That you were bound to win?

DES GRIEUX
Manon, I love you!

GUILLOT
It's time to stop the game!

DES GRIEUX
Whatever you desire.

GUILLOT
You are not fooling me, not in the
least!

DES GRIEUX
What's that?

GUILLOT
I prefer not to play
When it's impossible to win!

DES GIREUX (*angry*)
What did you say!

GUILLOT
So now you're angry!
Do you always pick a fight
With people you have robbed?

DES GRIEUX
You mean that I am cheating?
You are lying!

LESCAUT, POUSSETTE, JAVOTTE,
ROSETTE AND THE CROWD
Messieurs, no, no! Come, come,
Messieurs,
You should not lose your temper in
such a place as this!

GUILLOT
I call you to witness, Messieurs,
Mesdemoiselles!
(*to Manon and Des Grieux*)
As for you, you will hear from me,
and very soon!
(*Guillot goes out.*)

THE CROWD
A thing like this has never happened!
This man! . . . He tried to cheat
Here in this home of the elite.

LESCAUT (*interposing*)
Come, come, Messieurs, do be calm!
(*to Des Grieux*)
Oh what a mess, see what you've done!
(*to the Dealers*)
Now make your play, Messieurs!

MANON (*to Des Grieux*)
Come on! We'd better leave here right
away.

DES GRIEUX
No! If I leave now
What will they say?
These people will believe that he was
right,
They'll say that I'm a thief!
(*There is loud knocking at the door.*)

POUSSETTE, JAVOTTE AND ROSETTE
What now? There's someone at the
door!

THE CROWD
Quickly, quickly hide all the gold!

MANON
What now? Who can be knocking?
I'm trembling, I do not know why!

A VOICE (*offstage*)
Open . . . in the name of the King!

LES JOUEURS

Au jeu!

LESCAUT

Plus un louis, pas même une pistole!
Plus rien! ils m'ont volé, moi! moi!

GUILLOT (à *Des Grieux*)

Vous avez une chance folle.
Mille louis de plus!

DES GRIEUX

Soit, monsieur. Mille louis!

GUILLOT

J'ai perdu!

MANON

(*s'approchant des joueurs*)

Eh bien, gagnes-tu?

DES GRIEUX

(*lui montrant l'or et les bons de
caisse*)

Regarde!

MANON

C'est à nous?

DES GRIEUX

C'est à nous.

MANON

Je t'adore!

GUILLOT

Le double! Voulez-vous?

DES GRIEUX

C'est dit!

GUILLOT

Je perds encore.

MANON (à *Des Grieux*)

Je te l'avais bien dit que tu devais
gagner.

DES GRIEUX

Manon! Je t'aime!

GUILLOT

J'arrête la partie!

DES GRIEUX

C'est comme vous voudrez.

GUILLOT

Ce serait duperie de s'obstiner.

DES GRIEUX

Plaît-il?

GUILLOT

Il suffit, je m'entends;
Vous avez vraiment des talents!

DES GRIEUX

Que dites-vous?

GUILLOT

Quelle furie!
Vouloir encor battre les gens
Quand on les a volés!

DES GRIEUX

Infâme calomnie! Misérable!

LESCAUT, POUSSETTE, JAVOTTE,
ROSETTE, TOUT LE MONDE

Messieurs, voyons, voyons, messieurs!
Quand on est dans le monde il faut se
tenir mieux!

GUILLOT

Je vous prends à témoin, messieurs,
mesdemoiselles!
(à *Des Grieux et à Manon, mena-
çant*)
Pour vous deux, vous aurez bientôt de
nos nouvelles!

(*Il sort.*)

LE CHOEUR

La chose ne s'est jamais vue,
Non, non jamais, certainement
On n'a volé pareillement.
(*Au fond les croupiers répétent*: Mes-
sieurs, faites vos jeux.)

LESCAUT

Voyons, messieurs! Calmez vous!

(à *Des Grieux*)

Ah! quel ennui! Qu'avec-vous fait?
Faites vos jeux, Messieurs!

MANON (à *Des Grieux*)

Partons, je t'en supplie, partons vite.

DES GRIEUX

Non, sur ma vie!
Si je partais, peut-être croirait-on
Qu'en m'accusant cet homme avait
raison!
(*On frappe fortement à la porte.*)

POUSSETTE, JAVOTTE ET ROSETTE

Eh mais . . . qui frappe de la sorte?

LES JOUEURS

Vite, vite, cachez l'argent!

MANON

Qui frappe à cette porte?
Je tremble, je ne sais pourquoi . . .

UNE VOIX

Ouvrez! au nom du Roi!

LESCAUT

The police! Take to the roof!

(*Lescaut escapes.*)

(*Enter Guillot, a police officer and guardsmen.*)

GUILLOT (*pointing to Des Grieux*)

He is the man, and she is his accomplice.

MANON (*to Guillot*)

You sneak!

GUILLOT (*to Manon*)

I'm sorry, Mademoiselle,
But the game was a little too neat!

(*softly*)

I told you I would have my revenge.

(*to Des Grieux*)

I have my revenge, Messieur.
Perhaps you will find someone to console you . . .

DES GRIEUX

And for a start, I will find consolation
By throwing you out of the window!

GUILLOT (*avoiding him*)

Out of the window!

THE COUNT DES GRIEUX

(*stepping in front of his son and crossing his arms*)

And I? Do you mean to throw me too?

DES GRIEUX

My father! You, here! You!

MANON

His father!

THE COUNT

Oh, my son, have you no sense of honor?
What is the end of this to be?
Don't you know this affair is a story
That's told through all the town, even to me?
No matter how much you implore me,
I'll not forgive,
For it is I who must protect our name.

DES GRIEUX

Oh my father, I pray you, forgive me!
Won't you open your heart and be kind?
This remorse and regret will be mine evermore,
Oh, help me to restore my name!

MANON

Ah, I know! Now I know we'll be parted,
And my heart is cold at the thought!
Ah, what pain and disgrace are before me evermore,
Is my whole life to end in shame!

GUILLOT

Now I have my revenge,
What a swift and terrible revenge!
I'll not forgive!
It's now a matter for the law.

THE CROWD

See how sadly they weep!
She is so young!
Pardon! For so much beauty
Should deserve to be forgiven.

THE COUNT (*pointing to Des Grieux*)

Come and take him!

(*aside to Des Grieux*)

But soon I'll see that you are free.

DES GRIEUX (*indicating Manon*)

What of her?

GUILLOT (*interposing*)

They'll take her away
With all the other women like her.

DES GRIEUX

Keep away! I intend to defend her.

MANON (*overcome*)

I will die . . . of shame . . . Ah, be kind!

ACT FIVE

The road to Le Havre. Beside the dusty way there are wind-blown trees and a mound covered with brambles and weeds. A cross road can be seen, and the sea in the distance. It is evening.

DES GRIEUX

(*sitting on the ground alone*)

Manon! Ah, poor Manon!
Even now I can see you with all your wretched comrades,
As the cart approaches. Oh black pitiless heaven!
O God, is this the end?

(*Lescaut enters.*)

LESCAUT

Un exempt de police!
Gagnons vite le toit!

(*Guillot, Le Comte, Un Exempt,
Gardes*)

GUILLOT

Le coupable est Monsieur . . . et voilà
sa complice.

MANON

Misérable!

GUILLOT (*à Manon*)

Mille regrets, Mademoiselle . . .
Mais la partie était trop belle!
(*bas*)
Je vous avais, bien dit que je me
vengerais!
(*à Des Grieux*)
J'ai pris ma revanche, mon maître!
Il faudra vous en consoler . . .

DES GRIEUX

J'y tâcherai! Mais je vais commencer
Par vous jeter par la fenêtre!

GUILLOT (*se sauvant*)

Par la fenêtre!

LE COMTE DES GRIEUX

(*se plaçant devant lui et croisant les
bras*)
Et moi . . . M'y jetez-vous aussi?

DES GRIEUX

Mon père! Vous ici . . . Vous!

MANON

Son père!

LE COMTE

Oui, je viens t'arracher à la honte
Qui chaque jour grandit sur toi;
Insensé! vois-tu pas qu'elle monte,
Et va s'élever jusqu'à moi!
Et malgré ton regard qui m'implore,
Pas de pardon!
Je dois veiller sur notre honneur!

DES GRIEUX

Ah! comprends ce regard qui t'implore,
Qui voudrait fléchir ta rigueur.
Le remords, tu le vois, me dévore
A jamais ne peux-tu sauver mon
honneur!

MANON

O douleur! l'avenir nous sépare!
Et d'effroi mon coeur et tremblant!
Un tourment trop cruel me dévore
Est-ce donc fait de mon honneur!

GUILLOT

Me voilà donc vengé!
Ma vengeance est terrible, elle est
prompte.
Non! Pas de pitié!
Vous appartenez à la loi.

CHOEUR

Ah! Cedez a ses pleurs!
Pour sa jeunesse
Grâce! Tant de beauté
Mérite que l'on ait pitié!

LE COMTE (*montrant Des Grieux*)

Qu'on l'emmène!
(*à Des Grieux*)
Plus tard on vous délivrera.

DES GRIEUX

Mais elle?

GUILLOT

Le guet la conduira
Où l'on emmène ses pareilles!

DES GRIEUX

N'approchez pas, je saurai la défendre!
(*On le désarme.*)

MANON (*s'evanouissant*)

Ah! c'en est fait! . . . Je meurs. Grâce!

ACTE CINQUIÈME

*La route du Havre. Un chemin poud-
reux. Quelques arbres desséchés par
le vent de la mer; un talus à droite
où poussent des genêts, des ajoncs; au
fond un chemin creux; à l'horizon la
mer. C'est la fin du jour.*

DES GRIEUX (*assis sur le tertre*)

Manon! Pauvre Manon!
Je te vois enchaînée avec ces miséra-
bles!
Et la charrette passe! O cieux in-
exorables,
Faut-il désespérer?

(*allant fièvreusement à Lescaut*)

DES GRIEUX (*feverishly*)

No! He's here! Have all your men
make ready,
The guard's not far away, they soon
will be here.
Are all your men well armed? They
must be prepared to fight,
And we will set her free!

(*noticing Lescaut's silence*)

Tell me, is it all arranged, is everything prepared?
But why are you so silent?

LESCAUT (*with an effort*)

Monsieur le Chevalier . . .

DES GRIEUX

Speak up!

LESCAUT

I fear that all is lost.

DES GRIEUX

What!

LESCAUT

As soon as they saw the guns of the
soldiers,
My cowardly men ran away.

DES GRIEUX (*aghast*)

You lie! Heaven has taken pity on my
suffering.
Now's our chance, now's the time to
free her,
In a moment Manon should be here in
my arms!

LESCAUT (*sadly*)

How I wish that were true!

DES GRIEUX

Go away!

LESCAUT

Hit me!
When you're a soldier of the King,
He does not pay too well, and many a
decent man
Becomes a rascal who deserts you in
the time of need.

(*There is a sound of singing in the
distance.*)

DES GRIEUX

What is that?

LESCAUT (*taking a look*)

Here come the Guardsmen,
They're marching up the highway.

DES GRIEUX (*starting to rush out*)

Manon! Manon!

(*Lescaut restrains him.*)

I've nothing but my sword,
But you and I might make a fight of
it!

LESCAUT

And what fools we would be!

DES GRIEUX

Come on!

LESCAUT

We cannot win! Listen here,
I can show you a much better way!

DES GRIEUX

But how?

LESCAUT

Take my advice! Let's go!

DES GRIEUX

No, no!

LESCAUT

I'll fix it so you'll see Manon.

DES GRIEUX

Go where? When her poor heart is
crying:
"Come to me!" Let me stay!

LESCAUT

If you love Manon, come on!

DES GRIEUX

If I love her! . . . when I would gladly
die
If I could find a way to save her!

LESCAUT

Come on!

DES GRIEUX

When shall I see her?

LESCAUT

Right away!
(*He takes Des Grieux behind the
bushes.*)
(*The Guards enter, singing.*)

GUARDSMEN

Oh my captain true,
Are you weary too
As we march with you?
Oh, no! Oh, no!
Never, never!
With a horse to ride
And a drink inside,
I could march forever.
Oh my captain fine,
Do we get no wine today,
As we march away?

DES GRIEUX

Non! C'est lui! Prépare ton escorte!
Les archers sont là-bas . . . ils arrivent
  ici.
Tes hommes sont armés? Ils nous
  prêtent main forte,
Et nous la délivrons!

(*voyant que Lescaut ne lui répond
pas*)

Quoi? N'est-ce pas ainsi que tout est
  convenu?
Tu gardes le silence.

LESCAUT (*avec effort*)

Monsieur le chevalier . . .

DES GRIEUX

Eh bien?

LESCAUT

Je pense que tout est perdu!

DES GRIEUX

Quoi?

LESCAUT

Dès qu'au soleil ont lui
Les mousquets des archers, tous ces
  lâches ont fui!

DES GRIEUX (*éperdu*)

Tu mens! . . . Le ciel a pris pitié de
  ma souffrance!
C'est l'instant de la délivrance;
Tout à l'heure Manon va tomber dans
  mes bras!

LESCAUT (*tristement*)

Je ne vous trompe pas!

DES GRIEUX

Va-t'en!

LESCAUT

Frappez!
Que voulez-vous? On est soldat . . . le
  roi
Paie assez mal! Alors, bien malgré soi,
On devient un coquin, un homme abo-
  minable!

(*On entend un bruit lointain.*)

DES GRIEUX

Qu' est-ce là?

LESCAUT (*regardent*)

Ce sont eux, sans doute!
Je les vois sur la route!

DES GRIEUX (*voulant s'élancer*)

Manon! Manon! . . .

(*Lescaut l'arrête.*)

Je n'ai que mon épée,
Mais nous allons les attaquer tous deux!

LESCAUT

Quelle folle équipée!

DES GRIEUX

Allons!

LESCAUT

Vous la perdrez! Croyez-moi, il vaut
  mieux
Prendre un autre moyen.

DES GRIEUX

Lequel?

LESCAUT

Je vous en prie, partons!

DES GRIEUX

Non, non!

LESCAUT

Vous la verrez, je le promets!

DES GRIEUX

Partir!
Lorsque son coeur me crie:
"Viens à moi!" Non! jamais!

LESCAUT

Si vous l'aimez, venez!

DES GRIEUX

Ah! si je l'aime!
Quand je veux tout braver,
Quand je voudrais mourir pour elle!

LESCAUT

Venez!

DES GRIEUX

Quand la verrai-je?

LESCAUT

A l'instant même!

(*Il entraîne Des Grieux par la gauche.*)

LES ARCHERS (*chanson de marche*)

Capitaine, ô gué!
Es-tu fatigué,
De nous voir à pied,
Capitaine, au gué!
Mais non, La Ramée,
On n'est pas trop mal
Sur un bon cheval
Pour mener l'armée!
Marche, La Ramée.
Est-c' que je boirai,
Capitaine, ô gué!

A GUARDSMAN *(to the Sergeant)*
After singing, we need a drink.

SERGEANT
That's the least . . . there isn't much glory
In seeing off a crowd of fallen women.

GUARDSMEN
People make fun of us!

SERGEANT
What of it, it's our job.
What are the prisoners talking about down there?

A GUARDSMAN
Nothing much. They're not so noisy.
That sick one seems to be half dead.

SERGEANT
Which one?

A GUARDSMAN
The one who hides her face and cries
When anyone tries to talk with her.

SERGEANT
The one called Manon?

DES GRIEUX *(behind the bushes)*
Dear God!

LESCAUT *(holding him back)*
Quiet! Let me do it!
(to the Sergeant)
Hey, comrade!

SERGEANT
A soldier!

LESCAUT
It would be better to say . . . a friend.
(to Des Grieux)
Have you some money?
(to the Sergeant)
You're an obliging fellow, I'm sure.
I want you to do a favor.

SERGEANT
What kind?

LESCAUT
Nothing much. That poor girl you were discussing . . .
Let me speak to her for a moment!

SERGEANT
Why?

LESCAUT
She's related to me.

SERGEANT
I can't do it.

LESCAUT
Ah! *(He gives him some money.)*

SERGEANT
(glancing around to see if anyone is looking)
Well . . .

LESCAUT *(giving him more)*
Shall I insist?

SERGEANT
Maybe . . .

LESCAUT *(giving him still more)*
I insist!

SERGEANT
Well, since you insist so strongly, I'll do it!
(louder)
I'm not so tough as I look.
Bring her back to me in the village before nightfall!
Unchain her!

LESCAUT
Thank you, my friend, and bon voyage!

SERGEANT
Don't thank me by trying to take her away!

LESCAUT *(raising his hand)*
I take my solemn oath. Is that enough?

SERGEANT
No. Anyhow one of my men will be watching you
From not too far away.

LESCAUT
Thank you, my friend, and bon voyage!

SERGEANT *(to the men)*
Forward march!

DES GRIEUX *(hidden)*
Merciful God, I thank you!
(The Guardsmen sing the marching song as they leave.)
Manon! I shall see her!

LESCAUT
And soon, I hope, you can take her away.

DES GRIEUX
(pointing to the Guardsman who remains)
But what of that soldier?

UN ARCHER (*au sergent*)
Après chanter, il faut boire!

LE SERGENT
C'est bien le moins! . . . car ce n'est
pas la gloire d'escorter l'arme au bras
et de faire embarquer des demoiselles
sans vertu!

LES ARCHERS
C'est se moquer de nous!

LE SERGENT
N'importe! C'est le métier!
Et que disent là-bas les captives?

L'ARCHER
Oh! rien! Elles ne bougent pas!
L'une d'elle est déjà malade, à demi
morte.

LE SERGENT
Laquelle?

L'ARCHER
Eh! celle qui cachait
Son visage, et pleurait quand l'un de
nous cherchait à lui parler.

LE SERGENT
Manon, alors?

DES GRIEUX (*derrière de feuillage*)
O ciel!

LESCAUT (*le retenant*)
Silence! Laissez-moi faire . . .
(*Des Grieux donne sa bourse à Lescaut
et s'éloigne.—Lescaut s'avançant seul
vers le sergent.*)
Hé, camarade!

LE SERGENT
Un soldat! . . .

LESCAUT
Mieux, je pense, un ami! (*à Des
Grieux*) Avez-vous de l'argent? (*au
sergent*) Vous êtes obligeant,
J'en suis sûr! . . . Je viens donc récla-
mer un service . . .

LE SERGENT
Et lequel?

LESCAUT
C'est, rien que pour un instant,
De me laisser causer avec la pauvre
fille dont vous parliez . . .

LE SERGENT
Pourquoi?

LESCAUT
Je suis de sa famille.

LE SERGENT
Impossible!

LESCAUT
Ah!
(*Il lui donne une pièce de monnaie.*)

LE SERGENT
(*regardant si on l'a vu*)
Pourtant . . .

LESCAUT
(*nouvelle pièce d' argent*)
En insistant?

LE SERGENT
Peut-être.

LESCAUT (*lui donne la bourse*)
On insiste!

LE SERGENT
Ah! ma foi, si vous parlez en maî-
tre! . . .
(*haut*)
Accordé! . . . Je ne suis pas si noir
Que j'en ai l'air! . . . Là-bas est le vil-
lage,
Vous l'y ramènerez vous-même, avant
ce soir!
Détachez-la!

LESCAUT
Merci, mon cher, et bon voyage!

LE SERGENT
N'allez pas, pour me remercier,
Essayer de nous l'enlever!

LESCAUT (*levant la main*)
J'en fais mon grand serment, en faut-
il davantage?

LE SERGENT
Non, d'ailleurs quelqu'un restera,
Qui de loin vous surveillera!

LESCAUT
Merci, mon cher, et bon voyage!

LE SERGENT
(*après avoir donné un ordre à un
archer*)
En marche, allons!

DES GRIEUX (*caché*)
Merci, Dieu de bonté!
(*Reprise de la chanson de marche. Les
archers sortent.*)
Manon! je vais la voir!

LESCAUT
Et bientôt, je l'espère, vous pourrez
l'emmener!

DES GRIEUX
(*montrant l'archer laissé là par le sergent*)
Ce soldat?

LESCAUT

I'll take care of him!

(*He jingles the money which remains in the purse.*)

I did well not to give him all of it.

(*Manon enters. As she comes along the path to the mound, she seems overcome by fatigue. Her clothes are simple and poor. As she sees Des Grieux she cries out with joy and falls in his arms.*)

MANON

Oh! Des Grieux!

DES GRIEUX

Oh, Manon! Manon! Manon!

(*Suddenly and brusquely she frees herself from his arms and falls weeping at his feet.*)

You're weeping!

MANON

(*weeping, holding her head in her hands.*)

Yes! With shame for myself and with sorrow for you!

DES GRIEUX

Lift up your head and dream of the future!

We'll be happy once more.

MANON

Do not try to deceive me!

DES GRIEUX

No! They will never take you

Off to that distant land far across the sea!

I will take you away where we can be happy

And where we can be free!

(*Manon is silent.*)

Manon, why don't you speak?

MANON (*with infinite tenderness*)

Only now, my beloved,

Since I'm lost and alone,

Do I know just how kind

And how good you can be.

Forgive me now, have pity on me

For the harm I have done!

(*Des Grieux starts to interrupt her, but she stops him.*)

No! No! There is more . . .

My heart was so light and unruly,

I know that it was you I truly loved,

Yet I betrayed you.

DES GRIEUX

Do not speak of betrayal!

MANON

I cannot say, I cannot tell

Just why I could hurt and deceive you.

When I loved you so well,

Darling, how could I leave you!

DES GRIEUX

Manon!

MANON

How I hate myself when I think

Of the love that we knew! But I was untrue.

And I would give my life itself

If I could pay for the sorrow and pain

That I have brought to you.

Can you forgive?

DES GRIEUX

What have I to forgive,

When your dear loving heart

Is joined again to mine!

MANON

Joy returns like a flame that burns

All my sorrows away!

We shall be happy once again!

DES GRIEUX

Now, Manon, you shall be my wife,

Ah, Manon, from this hour

You are mine once again!

Heaven itself has forgiven you!

I love you!

MANON

Now I can die in peace.

DES GRIEUX

Die! No!

Live for me and my love!

You and I, free from danger,

Shall go on together

In happiness and peace.

MANON

(*as if in a dream, leaning on Des Grieux*)

I may once again be happy.

Let us dream of the past . . .

The inn . . . and the coach . . .and the shadowy road . . .

The letter you wrote . . . the little table . . . and your black robe at St. Sulpice . . .

See how well I remember?

LESCAUT

J'en fais mon affaire!

(faisant sonner ce qui reste dans la bourse)

J'ai très bien fait de ne pas tout donner.

MANON

(descend péniblement et comme brisée par la fatigue, le petit sentier tracé sur le talus; son costume est pauvre et simple, elle pousse un cri de joie en voyant Des Grieux et tombe dans ses bras.)

Ah! Des Grieux!

DES GRIEUX

O Manon! Manon! Manon!

(Tout à coup, brusquement, Manon se dégage des bras de Des Grieux, tombe et se prend à pleurer amèrement.)

Tu pleures!

MANON

(pleurant, la tête dans ses mains)

Oui, de honte sur moi, mais de douleur sur toi!

DES GRIEUX

Manon! Lève la tête et ne songe qu'aux heures
D'un bonheur qui revient!

MANON

Ah! pourquoi me tromper?

DES GRIEUX

Non, ces terres lointaines,
Dont ils te menaçaient, tu ne les verras pas!
Nous fuirons tous les deux! Au delà de ces plaines
Nous porterons nos pas!
      (Silence de Manon)
Manon, réponds-moi donc!

MANON

(avec une tendresse infinie)

Seul amour de mon âme!
Je ne sais qu'aujourd'hui la bonté de ton coeur,
Et si bas qu'elle soit, hélas! Manon réclame
Pardon, pitié pour son erreur!

(Des Grieux veut l'interrompre, elle lui met la main sur la bouche.)

Non! non! encore! Mon coeur fût léger et volage
Et, même en vous aimant
Eperdument, j'étais ingrate!

DES GRIEUX

Ah! pourquoi ce langage?

MANON

Et je ne puis m'imaginer
Comment, et par quelle folie,
J'ai pu vous chagriner
Un seul jour de ma vie!

DES GRIEUX

Assez!

MANON

Je me hais et maudis en pensant
A ces douces amours, par ma faute brisées,
Et je ne paierais pas assez de tout mon sang
La moitié des douleurs que je vous ai causées!
Pardonnez-moi!

DES GRIEUX

Qu'ai-je à te pardonner
Quand ton coeur à mon coeur vient de se redonner!

MANON

Ah! je sens une pure flamme
M'éclairer de ses feux.
Je vois enfin les jours heureux!

DES GRIEUX

Ah! Manon, mon amour, ma femme,
Oui, ce jour radieux
Nous unit tous les deux!
Le ciel lui-même
Te pardonne . . . Je t'aime!

MANON

Ah! je puis donc mourir!

DES GRIEUX

Mourir! non, vivre!
Et sans dangers désormais pouvoir suivre,
Deux à deux, ce chemin où tout va refleurir!

MANON

(comme dans un rêve s'appuyant sur Des Grieux)

Oui, je puis encore être heureuse.
Nous reparlerons du passé . . .
De l'auberge . . . du coche . . . et de la route ombreuse . . .
Du billet par ta main tracé
De la petite table . . . et de ta robe noire
A Saint-Sulpice! . . . Ah! j'ai bonne mémorie.

DES GRIEUX

It's a beautiful dream . . .
All is prepared to help us to escape!

MANON

I cannot breathe . . . I am fainting.
Escape? No! I cannot go on . . . go on
. . . any more . . .
A heavy sleep comes upon me,
A sleep with no awakening . . .

DES GRIEUX

You must be strong! The night is
  falling,
The evening star is shining.

MANON

Ah! It is like a diamond!
        (smiling)
You see, that is all I ever think of.

DES GRIEUX

It's time to go, Manon.

MANON (tenderly)

I love you!
And this kiss will be my last farewell . . .

DES GRIEUX

No, I will not believe it!
You shall not die! Remember me!
Is this not my hand,
Can't you feel it pressing?

MANON (as if falling to sleep)

Oh, do not wake me now . . .

DES GRIEUX

Are these not my arms tenderly
  caressing?

MANON

Oh, take me in your arms!

DES GRIEUX

Is it not my voice calling through my
tears?

MANON

Oh, do not speak of tears!

DES GRIEUX

The tender, happy memories . . .

MANON

Memories of remorse!

DES GRIEUX

That is all forgotten!

MANON

How can I forget the pain and sadness of our love!

MANON AND DES GRIEUX

Yes, it is your hand
Now I feel it pressing,
Ah, it is your voice!
Yes, these are your arms
Tenderly caressing,
Loving me once more!
We will love again
As we loved before!

MANON (failing)

I am dying . . .

DES GRIEUX

Manon!

MANON

Better so!
Now you know the story
Of Manon Lescaut . . .
        (She dies.)

END OF THE OPERA

DES GRIEUX

C'est un rêve charmant!
Tout s'apprête pour notre liberté!

MANON

Partons! Non . . . il m'est impossible
. . . d'avancer . . . davantage . . .
Je sens le sommeil que me gagne . . .
Un sommeil sans reveil!
J'étouffe! je succombe!

DES GRIEUX

Reviens à toi! . . . Voici la nuit qui
tombe!
C'est la première étoile! . . .

MANON (*regardant le ciel*)

Ah! le beau diamant!
(*souriant*)
Tu vois, je suis encore coquette!

DES GRIEUX

On vient! partons! Manon!

MANON
(*avec une tendresse infinie*)

Je t'aime!
Et ce baiser, c'est un adieu suprême!

DES GRIEUX

Non! . . . je ne veux pas croire! . . .
Ecoute-moi! Rappelle-toi!
N'est-ce plus ma main que cette main
presse?

MANON (*s'endormant*)

Ne me réveille pas!

DES GRIEUX

N'est-elle pour toi plus une caresse?

MANON

Berce-moi dans tes bras!

DES GRIEUX

Reconnais ma voix à travers mes larmes!

MANON

Oublions le passé!

DES GRIEUX

Souvenirs pleins des charmes . . .

MANON

O cruels remords!

DES GRIEUX

Je t'ai pardonné!

MANON

Ah! puis-je oublier les tristes jours de
nos amours!

DES GRIEUX

Tout est oublié.

MANON ET DES GRIEUX

Oui, c'est bien ta main
Que cette main presse!
Ah! c'est bien ta voix!
N'est-elle pour toi plus une caresse,
Tout comme autrefois!
Bientôt renaîtra le bonheur passé!

MANON (*comme s'endormant*)

Ah! Je meurs!

DES GRIEUX

Manon!

MANON

Il le faut!
Et c'est là l'histoire
De Manon Lescaut!

(*Elle meurt.*)

FIN